UNITED NATIONS ECONOMIC COMMISSION FOR EUROPE

Guidance on Land-Use Planning, the Siting of Hazardous Activities and related Safety Aspects

Note

Symbols of United Nations documents are composed of capital letters combined with figures. Mention of such a symbol indicates a reference to a United Nations document.

The designations employed and the presentation of the material in this publication do not imply the expression of any legal opinion whatsoever on the part of the Secretariat of the United Nations concerning the legal status of any country, territory, city or area, or of its authorities, or concerning the delimitation of its frontiers or boundaries. In particular, the boundaries shown on the map do not imply official endorsement or acceptance by the United Nations.

This volume is issued in English, French and in Russian.

United Nations publication issued by United Nations Economic Commission for Europe.

The United Nations Economic Commission for Europe would like to thank the European Investment Bank, the EU bank, for their support to the *Guidance on Land-use Planning, the Siting of Hazardous Activities and related Safety Aspects*.

ECE/CP.TEIA/35

UNITED NATIONS PUBLICATION
Sales No: E.18.II.E.6 ISBN: 978-92-1-117151-8 e-ISBN: 978-92-1-363050-1

Background and acknowledgements

In response to the need to improve cooperation and coordination between land-use planning and industrial safety procedures, the United Nations Economic Commission for Europe (UNECE) decided to develop a guidance on land-use planning, the siting of hazardous activities and related safety aspects under three UNECE instruments — the Convention on the Transboundary Effects of Industrial Accidents (Industrial Accidents Convention), the Convention on Environmental Impact Assessment in a Transboundary Context (Espoo Convention) and its Protocol on Strategic Environmental Assessment (Protocol on SEA).

In 2014, the Conference of the Parties to the Industrial Accidents Convention adopted a workplan for 2015–2016, which included an activity on the sharing of good practices and development of guidance on safety and land-use planning. It was agreed to carry out this activity in cooperation with the Protocol on SEA to the Espoo Convention and the UNECE Committee on Housing and Land Management, with the support of the European Investment Bank, the EU bank. The guidance was expected to explain how the notion of land-use plans and programmes used in other relevant legal instruments applied to the Industrial Accidents Convention's provisions on the siting of hazardous activities. In 2015, the Working Group on Environmental Impact Assessment and Strategic Environmental Assessment (Working Group on EIA and SEA) under the Espoo Convention and its Protocol on SEA agreed to include the activity in the workplan for 2014–2016, with a view to promoting synergies with the Industrial Accidents Convention.

Three UNECE instruments — Industrial Accidents Convention, Espoo Convention and its Protocol on SEA — address issues related to land-use planning, the siting and modification of hazardous activities from different perspectives.

Parties to the Industrial Accidents Convention are obliged to ensure that operators of hazardous facilities reduce risks and demonstrate the safe performance of these facilities, and competent authorities shall carry out regular inspections and issue licences or bans. Parties shall seek the establishment of policies for the siting and significant modification of hazardous activities and land-use planning in the broader context, taking account of transboundary risks. The Espoo Convention is a key instrument to bring together all stakeholders to prevent transboundary environmental damage before it occurs, through environmental impact assessment of planned activities, including industrial and chemical installations and thermal and nuclear plants. The Protocol on SEA augments the Espoo Convention by ensuring that individual Parties integrate environmental and health considerations into their economic development or land-use plans and programmes at the earliest stages, providing for extensive public participation in the governmental decision-making process. While negotiated in the framework of UNECE, the Protocol on SEA is open for accession by non-UNECE States and the Espoo Convention in the process of becoming a global instrument.

In accordance with the respective mandates, the guidance was developed jointly under the Industrial Accidents Convention, the Espoo Convention and the Protocol on SEA, in cooperation with the UNECE Committee on Housing and Land Management, with the support of the European Investment Bank, the EU bank. It is comprised of two parts — general guidance (Part A) and technical guidance (Part B). The guidance was drafted by consultants to the UNECE secretariat: Mr. Lorenzo van Wijk, expert on land-use planning and the siting of hazardous activities, Mr. Jerzy Jendroska, legal expert, and Mr. Jiri Dusik, environmental assessment expert.

A draft version of the guidance was considered by the Working Group on the Development of the Convention of the Industrial Accidents Convention and by the Working Group on EIA and SEA under the Espoo Convention and its Protocol on SEA during a joint workshop held in Geneva on 13 April 2016. The Working Group on EIA and SEA further revised the draft guidance at its meeting in November 2016. The Conference of the Parties to the Industrial Accidents Convention at its ninth meeting (Ljubljana, 28-30 November 2016) took note of the guidance (Parts A and B), and entrusted the Bureau with its finalization on the basis of the points raised at the meeting and also the comments of the subsidiary body to the Espoo Convention and its Protocol. The Meetings of the Parties to the Espoo Convention and the Protocol on SEA endorsed the general part of the guidance (Part A) and took note of its technical part (Part B) at their seventh and third sessions, respectively (Minsk, 13-16 June 2017). The governing bodies encouraged countries to promote the implementation of the guidance among land-use planners, environmental assessment experts and industrial safety specialists. They also requested the relevant body secretariats to publish it.

The secretariat of the Industrial Accidents Convention and the Espoo Convention and its Protocol on SEA ensured the review of the guidance and its finalization, which was possible, thanks to the contributions by Tea Aulavuo, Nicolas Bonvoisin, Olga Carlos, Amy Edgar, Franziska Hirsch, Claudia Kamke, Alma Nurmaldina, Gaelle Rigo, Yelyzaveta Rubach, Aphrodite Smagadi and Rebecca Wardle.

Foreword

Industry plays a crucial role in our everyday lives by providing jobs and delivering a wide range of materials, products and services. Yet, rarely do we think about the hazardous substances that are stored, processed or produced at industrial facilities and the severe consequences that their accidental release into the soil, air or water may have on our lives, the environment and economies. The devastating impacts of such disasters, including in a transboundary context, have been demonstrated by major industrial accidents within and beyond the United Nations Economic Commission for Europe (UNECE) region over the past decades. Most of us surely remember or have heard about the accidents at the Sandoz storehouse in Switzerland (1986), the Ajka aluminium refinery in Hungary (2010) or the Buncefield explosion in the United Kingdom (2005). The effects of such accidents are often more severe if coordination between industrial safety experts and land-use planning authorities was lacking to ensure, for example, appropriate safety distances. The Tianjin disaster in China (2015) has demonstrated the severe impacts of an accident in a storage facility on the surrounding densely populated area and its homes and schools. The present Guidance on Land-use Planning, the Siting of Hazardous Activities and related Safety Aspects has been developed to avoid and minimize the adverse impacts of such accidents on our communities and environment — if they do occur.

Safety and environmental considerations must come first in decisions on the use of land, and the location of industrial hazardous activities. It is of utmost importance to ensure that appropriate safety measures are in place at industrial facilities, and that they are not constructed in areas prone to natural disasters and other risks, which are likely to be exacerbated by the expected increase of extreme weather events due to climate change. Assessing the potential environmental and health risks posed by hazardous industrial facilities, raising awareness of these risks, and identifying the safest and most sustainable alternatives, in a cross-sectoral dialogue, is crucial in this regard. There is thus an ongoing need for greater integration of industrial safety, land-use planning and environmental assessment procedures — to be able to make coordinated decisions on accident prevention and risk reduction. As such, this guidance supports countries in their efforts to implement the Sendai Framework for Disaster Risk Reduction 2015-2030 and the 2030 Agenda for Sustainable Development with its Sustainable Development Goals.

Three UNECE legal instruments — the Convention on the Transboundary Effects of Industrial Accidents, the Convention on Environmental Impact Assessment in a Transboundary Context and its Protocol on Strategic Environmental Assessment — address issues related to land-use planning and the siting of hazardous activities from different perspectives. In light of the need for better integration between the different communities, the three UNECE instruments worked together with the European Investment Bank, the EU bank to develop guidance on land-use planning, the siting of hazardous activities and related safety aspects. The guidance shares examples and points to good practices of countries' efforts in the UNECE region to integrate industrial accidents safety considerations into environmental assessment and land-use planning processes.

I encourage public authorities, industry experts, environmental assessment practitioners, facility operators and other relevant stakeholders to make extensive use of this guidance for improving safety and sustainability at hazardous facilities, siting decisions, and land-use planning around these facilities. I look forward to the successful implementation of the guidance across the UNECE region and beyond, so as to limit the number of industrial accidents and minimise consequences for human health and the environment.

Olga Algayerova
Executive Secretary
United Nations Economic Commission for Europe

Contents

Part A - General Guidance on Land-Use Planning, the Siting of Hazardous Activities and related Safety Aspects

List of tables

List of boxes

Contents

Part B - Technical Guidance on Land-Use Planning, the Siting of Hazardous Activities and related Safety Aspects

Part A
General Guidance on Land-Use Planning, the Siting of Hazardous Activities and related Safety Aspects

I. Introduction

A. Objective

1. The primary purpose of the guidance is to assist Parties[1] in more effectively mitigating the effects of possible industrial accidents and the consequences on human health, the environment and cultural heritage within countries and across borders. The guidance aims to achieve this by:

    a. Clarifying the relevant provisions of the Convention on the Transboundary Effects of Industrial Accidents (Industrial Accidents Convention), the Protocol on Strategic Environmental Assessment (Protocol on SEA) and the Convention on Environmental Impact Assessment in a Transboundary Context (Espoo Convention);

    b. Highlighting the synergies and interlinkages between these instruments;

    c. Providing examples of good practice and integrated approaches to implementing the provisions related to land-use planning, safety and hazardous industrial activities.

2. The Industrial Accidents Convention primarily deals with prevention of, preparedness for, and response to industrial accidents, with a view to reducing the risks of accidents and, when they do occur, their effects. The Protocol on SEA and the Espoo Convention ensure the assessment of the potential adverse impacts on environment and health of land-use planning and the siting of hazardous activities. It is therefore important that the practices of land-use planning and the siting of hazardous activities, which are dealt with through the provisions of the Protocol on SEA and the Espoo Convention, respectively, are integrated with practices under the Industrial Accidents Convention.

3. Over the years, the practical implementation of these legal instruments has faced many challenges within and between countries. Accordingly, the present guidance intends to support public authorities and practitioners in applying their provisions in relation to land-use planning, safety and hazardous industrial activities.

4. The public authorities and practitioners that this guidance aims to support include: decision makers and policymakers at the national and local levels; proponents/developers and operators; and those who provide technical support in the fields of urban planning, environmental assessment or industrial accident risk management. It is not intended to be a detailed, hands-on instruction manual, but rather a source of advice on the right procedures and processes for cooperation within and between Parties.

5. It is recommended that public authorities and practitioners take into account the provisions of the above-mentioned instruments in their decisions, including strategic environmental assessment (SEA) and environmental impact assessment (EIA) decisions, about:

    a. Land-use plans or programmes;

    b. Plans to site potentially hazardous activities;

    c. Permits that authorize activities (including hazardous industrial activities) or significant modifications of these activities on specific sites.

6. The information and views set out in this guidance do not create any obligations and are without prejudice to existing obligations set out in the Industrial Accidents Convention, the Espoo Convention and the Protocol on SEA.

---

1 Parties to the Industrial Accidents Convention, the Protocol on SEA and/or the Espoo Convention.

7. With regard to the references to the European Union legislation, this guidance does not create any obligation on the European Union member States, and its recommendations are without prejudice to the obligations set out in the respective European Union legislation.

B. Methodology and scope

8. The guidance has been drafted by a consultant to the European Investment Bank based on:
    a. A desktop review of general documentation and informational material;
    b. An analysis of the 27 responses to a survey of national authorities of the relevant treaties, and interested stakeholders, conducted from 21 December 2015 to 18 January 2016. The survey identified the needs, existing good practices and lessons learned regarding the application of the relevant provisions of those instruments;[2]
    c. Inputs from a legal expert and an SEA practitioner;
    d. Support from a small group of experts on land-use planning;
    e. Detailed comments from Parties.

9. A first draft of the guidance was presented at a joint workshop on 13 April 2016, in the context of the seventh meeting of the Working Group on the Development of the Industrial Accidents Convention (Geneva 12–14 April 2016) and the fifth meeting of the Working Group on EIA and SEA (Geneva, 11–15 April 2016).[3] Following comments by workshop participants and the Working Groups, the draft was finalized for submission to the Conference of Parties to the Industrial Accidents Convention at its ninth meeting (Ljubljana, 28–30 November 2016) and the Working Group on EIA and SEA at its sixth meeting (Geneva, 7–10 November), with a view to its subsequent submission to the seventh and third sessions, respectively, of the governing bodies of the Espoo Convention and the Protocol on SEA.

10. Originally, the activity was expected to focus on land-use planning and the application of the Protocol on SEA. However, it became apparent that, while land-use plans are subject to an SEA procedure, decisions on the siting of hazardous activities are subject to an EIA procedure and therefore the Espoo Convention was of relevance. Furthermore, several aspects covered by the Aarhus Convention were also considered.

C. Structure of the guidance

11. The guidance is composed of two parts. Part A is the guidance on general matters, which provides support and clarification to public authorities and practitioners on the requirements, interlinkages and application of the relevant United Nations Economic Commission for Europe (UNECE) instruments. Part B is the technical guidance on land-use planning and the siting of hazardous activities and related safety aspects, which focuses on the risk aspects of hazardous facilities.

12. Chapter II below outlines the main interlinkages, synergies and complementarities between the relevant UNECE instruments. Chapter III shares Parties' practices in implementing the provisions related to industrial accidents, safety, EIA, SEA and consultation of the relevant authorities. Finally, chapter IV constitutes the core guidance document. It provides guidance on general aspects of the instruments, and is complemented by a table with practical advice.

---

2   The full results of the survey are set out in the first draft of the guidance, Part A, Annex, available from the Industrial Accidents Convention website at http://www.unece.org/environmental-policy/conventions/industrial-accidents/envteiaguidelines/envteialup.html.

3   See ECE/MP.EIA/WG.2/2016/2, paras. 41–46 and annex, and ECE/CP.TEIA/WG.1/2016/2, paras. 17–18 and annex II, respectively.

II. Interlinkages, synergies and complementarities between relevant legal instruments

13. The Industrial Accidents Convention promotes international cooperation in relation to industrial accidents capable of causing transboundary effects. Parties undertake measures to identify hazardous activities within their jurisdiction, consult with and notify each other, prevent such accidents and ensure that the public in the areas capable of being affected by an industrial accident is informed and provided with an opportunity to participate in procedures relating to prevention and preparedness measures.

14. With regard to the planning and safety of hazardous activities, Parties should not only consider the Industrial Accidents Convention, but also the Protocol on SEA and the Espoo and Aarhus Conventions. A majority of Parties to the Industrial Accidents Convention are also Parties to one or more of the other relevant UNECE instruments. The treaties only rarely make direct reference to each other (e.g., Industrial Accidents Convention, article 4, para. 4; and Protocol on SEA, article 15), but in practice there are important interlinkages between the instruments that are recommended to be taken into account when designing national policies where appropriate plans, programmes, or projects.

15. The primary functions of the relevant UNECE legal instruments and their key interlinkages are outlined in table 1.

Table 1 - Primary function and interlinkages of selected legal instruments

Instrument	Broad objective	Relevance to land-use planning, safety and hazardous industrial activities	Key interlinkages
Industrial Accidents Convention	To prevent the occurrence of industrial accidents as far as possible, to mitigate or minimize their impacts and to promote active international cooperation between countries before, during and after an industrial accident.	Prevention and minimization of industrial accidents and their effects.	Environmental and health risks identified in SEA and EIA procedures for land-use planning and siting of hazardous activities can be used to inform industrial safety planning under the Industrial Accidents Convention.
Protocol on SEA	To provide for a high level of protection of the environment, including health, by: (a) ensuring that environmental, including health, considerations are thoroughly taken into account in the development of plans and programmes; (b) contributing to the consideration of environmental, including health, concerns in the preparation of policies and legislation; (c) establishing clear, transparent and effective procedures for SEA; (d) providing for public participation in SEA; and (e) integrating by these means environmental, including health, concerns into measures and instruments designed to further sustainable development.	Informing decisions on land-use plans and programmes.	Data on industrial safety generated and exchanged under the Industrial Accidents Convention is recommended to be used to address environmental and health risks identified in SEA procedures for land-use plans or programmes under the Protocol.
Espoo Convention	To ensure international cooperation in assessing and managing environmental impacts of proposed activities in a transboundary context.	Informing decisions on the siting of hazardous activities.	Data on industrial safety that is generated and exchanged under the Industrial Accidents Convention is recommended to be used to address environmental and health risks identified in EIA procedures for making decisions or authorizing permits for hazardous activities under the Espoo Convention.
Aarhus Convention	To guarantee the rights of access to information, public participation in decision-making and access to justice in environmental matters, in order to contribute to the protection of the right of every person of present and future generations to live in an environment adequate to his or her health and well-being.	Public participation, access to information and access to justice in the process of EIA, SEA and industrial safety planning procedures.	The public should be meaningfully engaged in the EIA, SEA and industrial safety planning procedures and decision-making.

16. The following areas where important interlinkages exist between the Industrial Accidents Convention, the Protocol on SEA, the Espoo Convention and, where relevant, the Aarhus Convention, are discussed in more detail below:

    a.   Addressing hazardous activities;

    b.   Screening;

    c.   Scoping;

    d.   Environmental report;[4]

    e.   Access to information, public participation and access to justice;

    f.   Transboundary procedure;

    g.   Decisions;

    h.   Monitoring.

A. Addressing hazardous activities

17. All four treaties contain mechanisms to address hazardous activities. A hazardous activity under the Industrial Accidents Convention is "any activity in which one or more hazardous substances are present or may be present in quantities at or in excess of the threshold quantities listed in annex I hereto, and which is capable of causing transboundary effects" (article 1, subpara. (b)). Annex I to that Convention provides a list of hazardous substances to define hazardous activities.

18. Although the Espoo Convention does not define "hazardous activity", it defines a proposed activity as "any activity or any major change to an activity subject to a decision of a competent authority in accordance with an applicable national procedure" (article 1, subpara. (v); see also appendix I). According to the Protocol on SEA, an SEA is obligatory for plans and programmes prepared for town and country planning or land-use that set the framework for future development consent for projects (article 4, para. 2, and annex I). The list of projects in the Protocol's annex I is similar to the list of activities in appendix I to the Espoo Convention. These activities, listed under the Protocol's annex 1 and assessed under an EIA in accordance with the Espoo Convention should also include, where applicable, hazardous activities in the meaning of the Industrial Accidents Convention.

19. The Aarhus Convention refers to decisions on "specific activities" (see article 6).[5] Activities under annex I (activities determined by national law to have a significant effect on the environment) require a public participation procedure. Such a procedure is also required for plans and programmes relating to the environment (article 7). For siting decisions or plans or programmes relating to hazardous activities, public participation under the Aarhus Convention may be required.

B. Screening

20. Screening of plans and programmes other than those defined in article 4, paragraph 2, of the Protocol on SEA is undertaken at the beginning of an environmental assessment to determine whether a full assessment or procedure is formally required under the relevant regulations. Screening is key to identify activities capable of causing transboundary effects.[6]

---

4 The terminology of the Espoo Convention differs slightly. For the purposes of this guidance, "environmental report" also refers to the EIA documentation (here, the EIA environmental report).

5 *The Aarhus Convention: An Implementation Guide* (second edition) suggests that the term is similar to "proposed activity" under the Espoo Convention (United Nations publication, Sales No. E.13.II.E.3, p. 131).

6 By its decision 2000/3, the Conference of the Parties to the Industrial Accidents Convention adopted Guidelines Facilitating the Identification of Hazardous Activities (ECE/CP.TEIA/2, annex IV) as later amended by decision 2004/2 (ECE/CP.TEIA/12, annex II).

21. Under the Industrial Accidents Convention, screening is not stipulated. However, the definition of "hazardous activities" in article 1, subparagraph (b), as expanded in annex I, implies a similar process to screening and could be considered during the screening procedures under EIA and SEA.

22. To determine whether a plan or programme (other than those defined in article 4, para. 2, of the Protocol on SEA) is likely to have significant environmental, including health, effects, Parties to the Protocol carry out screening (article 4, paras. 3–4). Screening is done either through a case-by-case examination or by specifying types of plans and programmes, or by combining both approaches (as outlined in article 5).

23. The Espoo Convention does not specify a screening procedure, but its appendix III, on general criteria to assist in the determination of the environmental significance of activities, provides screening criteria. These include a number of factors that are relevant to the safety aspects of hazardous activities, such as general references to risk, size, location and effects.

24. In sum, all three instruments include either a formal screening process or a similar process to identify activities (including those capable of causing transboundary effects) to be addressed in EIA, SEA and industrial safety planning procedures.

C. Scoping

25. Scoping is the process of identifying the precise and case-specific scope of information needed to be included in the EIA documentation or environmental report to be submitted to the competent authority. Scoping requires that the environmental report reflect the information needs of the decision-making body and determines the topics to be considered as well as the depth or detail of the information to be presented on each topic.

26. The Industrial Accidents Convention does not specifically outline the scope of the information to be provided, as it is recognized that "the analysis and evaluation of the hazardous activity should be performed with a scope and to a depth which vary depending on the purpose for which they carried out" (annex V, para. 1). However, annex V, paragraph 2 lists "matters which should be considered in the analysis and evaluation", in relation to emergency planning (items 1–5), decision-making on siting (items 6–8 in addition to 1–5), information to the public (item 9, in addition to 1–4) and prevention measures (items 10–16 in addition to 1–9).

27. Appendix II to the Espoo Convention provides guidance on the minimum content of the environmental report, including a description of the proposed activity, reasonable alternatives, the potential environmental impact of the proposed activity, the mitigation measures and monitoring and management programmes.

28. Article 6 of the Protocol on SEA sets out the scoping procedure. It establishes the arrangements for determining the relevant information to be included in the environmental report and the authorities to be consulted, as well as opportunities for public participation. Article 7 sets out the content of the environmental report, which the proponent prepares for consultation among authorities, public participation and possibly also transboundary consultations.

D. Environmental report

29. The Industrial Accidents Convention does not stipulate that an environmental report must be prepared. However, it does require that Parties exchange information, consult each other and undertake cooperative measures. Data on industrial safety that are generated and exchanged under the Convention (under article 15) are recommended to be used to address environmental and health risks in land-use plans and siting decisions, e.g., in SEA and EIA environmental reports. Moreover, measures envisaged in the off-site contingency plans prepared for hazardous activities can be included in the SEA environmental report (see article 8, para. 3).

30. Under the Protocol on SEA and Espoo Convention, an environmental report must be prepared and submitted to the competent authority. The environmental report requirements are similar under these two instruments (see sect. C above).

31. Safety aspects of hazardous activities can be addressed in SEA environmental reports in relation to plans or programmes (i.e., land-use plans), in order to fulfil the requirements of the Industrial Accidents Convention.

32. In addition, safety aspects of siting hazardous activities can be addressed in EIA environmental reports in relation to decisions and permits authorizing hazardous activities (projects) on specific sites.

E. Access to information, public participation and access to justice

33. In adopting land-use plans or siting decisions, Parties to the Industrial Accidents Convention have to abide by specific obligations relating to the free exchange of information between Parties or between Parties and other stakeholders, such as the public (see articles 9 and 15 and annexes XI and IV, item 5). Article 9 of that Convention also regulates public participation and access to justice issues in relation to matters covered by the Convention, without further detailing the procedures.

34. Similarly, the Espoo Convention (article 4) and its Protocol (article 5, para. 4, and articles 9 and 10) require Parties to provide for access to information by obliging them to share documentation with other Parties and the public for transboundary consultation purposes and public participation procedures. Both instruments provide for public participation and grant rights for the public to be informed, to express their views and to have those views taken into account. In a transboundary context, the public of affected Parties must have an opportunity to participate that is equivalent to the opportunity provided to the public of the Party of origin (see Espoo Convention, article 2, paras. 2 and 6, article 3, para. 8, and article 4, para. 2; and the Protocol on SEA, article 8).

35. The Aarhus Convention is generally the instrument of reference regarding access to information, public participation and access to justice in environmental matters. Its provisions should be observed by Parties to the Industrial Accidents Convention, the Protocol on SEA and the Espoo Convention that are also party to the Aarhus Convention to complement the basic obligations on access to information, public participation and access to justice arising from those instruments. At the same time, the provisions of the Industrial Accidents Convention also complement the obligations of the Aarhus Convention. Specifically, article 9 of the Industrial Accidents Convention requires that adequate information is given to the public in the areas capable of being affected by an industrial accident, and that they are given an opportunity to participate in relevant procedures and have access to relevant administrative and judicial proceedings.

F. Transboundary procedure

36. The Industrial Accidents and Espoo Conventions have similar transboundary procedures. The Industrial Accidents Convention (article 4, para. 4) specifically refers to the Espoo Convention:

> When a hazardous activity is subject to an environmental impact assessment in accordance with the [Espoo Convention] and that assessment includes an evaluation of the transboundary effects of industrial accidents …, the final decision taken for the purposes of [that Convention] shall fulfil the relevant requirements of this [Industrial Accidents] Convention.

37. There is no formal link between the transboundary procedures of the Industrial Accidents Convention and the Protocol on SEA. However, article 10 of the Protocol requires transboundary consultations between Parties, which are triggered when one Party is developing a plan or programme that has the potential to cause significant transboundary environmental, including health, effects.

G. Decisions

38. Safety aspects of hazardous activities are recommended to be addressed in plans or programmes addressing land use or in decisions or permits authorizing activities or significant modifications of these activities on specific sites (siting decisions). Under the Industrial Accidents Convention, article 7 requires that Parties seek to establish policies on siting of hazardous activities and their modifications, as well as policies on significant developments in areas that may be affected by the transboundary effects of an industrial accident arising out of a hazardous activity. Annex VI, pursuant to article 7, outlines the matters that should be taken into consideration when making siting decisions, such as: the results of risk analysis and evaluation; consultations and public participation processes; environmental risk evaluations and any transboundary effects; and the siting of hazardous activities.

39. The Protocol on SEA also contains requirements for decision-making. Parties to the Protocol could undertake an SEA when developing plans, programmes, or, where appropriate, policies, that influence the siting of hazardous activities in order to identify and incorporate environmental and health considerations at the earliest stage possible. Under article 11, when a plan or programme is being adopted, the conclusions of the environmental report, measures to prevent, reduce or mitigate adverse effects and comments received during the process, must be taken into consideration.

40. Similarly, a transboundary EIA can inform and analyse siting decisions for hazardous activities. Article 6 of the Espoo Convention seeks to ensure that the final decision on the siting of a proposed activity (which may include a hazardous activity) takes into account the outcome of the EIA, the assessment documentation (environmental report), the comments received and the outcome of the consultations during the EIA process. In addition, under article 4, paragraph 4, of the Industrial Accidents Convention, when a hazardous activity is subject to an EIA in accordance with the Espoo Convention and it involves transboundary effects, the final decision on the EIA must fulfil the relevant requirements of the Industrial Accidents Convention.

H. Monitoring

41. Regarding monitoring, the Industrial Accidents Convention promotes the exchange of information between Parties, operators and competent authorities as part of multilateral and bilateral cooperation. This cooperation includes the sharing of programmes for monitoring, planning, research and development, as well as the methods used for the prediction of risks, including criteria for the monitoring and assessment of transboundary effects (see annex XI).

42. Both the Protocol on SEA (article 12) and the Espoo Convention (appendices II and V) envisage monitoring the actual effects of the plans or activities that have undergone environmental assessment. As stated above, the results of monitoring (relevant to hazardous industrial activities) are recommended to be shared between Parties, operators and competent authorities to fulfil the requirements of the Industrial Accidents Convention.

III. Experiences and good practices of member States based on the survey findings

43. Over the past twenty to thirty years, EIA and SEA procedures have been used to ensure that potential environmental impacts arising from plans, programmes and projects are identified and assessed at the earliest stage possible, and subsequently communicated to the decision maker, minimized and monitored. An important part of the process is to provide opportunities for the public to be meaningfully involved. SEA addresses both development and conservation objectives, as they are applied to land-use plans and programmes, which set the framework for many development projects that, individually or cumulatively, may cause significant adverse effects on the environment and human health. Similarly, EIA addresses development and conservation objectives, as they are applied to projects, such as the siting of hazardous activities.

44. There are many examples of Parties' efforts to coordinate or integrate the overlapping and interlinked assessment obligations for a siting decision related to EIA, land-use planning related to SEA and industrial accidents analyses and evaluations. Box 1 below provides examples of integrated procedures that were gathered through the survey.

45. Good-practice examples of a fully integrated process of industrial safety planning, EIA and SEA are found in Bulgaria, Belgium (Flanders Region) and Portugal, as shown in boxes 2, 3 and 4 below. The competent safety authorities — the competent authorities for the purposes of the Industrial Accidents Convention — of the United Kingdom of Great Britain and Northern Ireland and Estonia have demonstrated particularly good practice in ensuring the inclusion of safety considerations in their land-use plans and siting decisions, as shown in boxes 5 and 6.

Box 1 - Integrated procedures for environmental impact assessment, strategic environmental assessment and analyses and evaluations related to industrial accidents safety in land-use planning

Armenia

The Armenian Law on EIA and Appraisal requires the inclusion of a description of the main risks of potential accidents in EIA reports.

Austria

The relevant requirements of the Protocol on SEA are integrated into land-use planning procedures in Austria. Risks and safety aspects relevant to the SEA procedure are considered on an individual basis. In certain cases, these aspects may influence the development of alternatives, mitigation measures or other SEA-related steps.

Bulgaria

The Environmental Protection Act of Bulgaria considers industrial accidents safety in both SEA and EIA instruments. The Act includes the main stages of the EIA procedure for EIA coordinated with the Seveso III Directive.[7] The Minister of Environment and Water identifies the SEA procedures to be carried out in order to ensure safe distances around hazardous facilities.

Estonia

In Estonia, the Chemicals Act requires an assessment of the hazards and risks relating to a facility when SEA or EIA is performed in the planning and design phase and that the public is informed during these proceedings.

Finland

In Finland, impact studies and reports addressing socioeconomic, social, cultural and other impacts must support proposed land-use plans. The entire area where a material impact is expected following the plan's implementation must be assessed. For certain areas, a separate comprehensive industrial safety assessment is undertaken alongside land-use planning.

---

7 Directive 2012/18/EU of the European Parliament and of the Council of 4 July 2012 on the control of major-accident hazards involving dangerous substances, amending and subsequently repealing Council Directive 96/82/EC.

Sweden

Under Swedish law, all accidents are considered to lead to environmental consequences — e.g., impacts on humans, property or cultural heritage or causing air, water or soil pollution. Potential impacts are described under the EIA or SEA with sufficient detail necessary for siting or land-use plan decision-making. All reasonable preventive measures to reduce any environmental impacts are addressed. The activity permit might be severely limited or not issued when preventive and mitigation measures are deemed insufficient to minimize damage caused by accidents.

United Kingdom

The likely impact of plans, programmes or projects on human health and/or the environment are issues that should be considered, where relevant, as part of an EIA or SEA in the United Kingdom. The impacts include those resulting from accidents.

Box 2 - Bulgaria: safety considerations as criteria for screening land-use plans determining the use of small areas at local level

The Minister of Environment and Water (for national plans) and Directors of Regional Inspectorates of Environment and Water (for local plans) are the competent environmental authorities in Bulgaria for SEA regarding land-use plans. They perform the following screening tests.

For land-use plans for siting of facilities, these authorities:

    a.   Check whether the investment proposal was subject to EIA. If so, they check whether the dangerous substances, major accidents risks and measures for prevention, control and limitation of consequences of major accidents for the environment and human health were evaluated and documented;

    b.   Check whether a safety report was adopted;

    c.   Verify safety distances from the facility to residential, public use or recreational areas, and transport routes.

If the conditions in (a)–(c) are all met, then, as a rule, SEA is not required. If they are not all met, an EIA must be conducted. A detailed development plan and land-use change cannot be adopted until safety distances are ensured.

For land-use plans for new residential or public use areas, or transport routes, these authorities:

    a.   Inform the developer of the presence and location of any existing facilities on the territory of the plan or plan modifications, including the risk potential of the facilities, permitted activities and the type and maximum allowed quantities of dangerous substances. For enterprises with high-risk potential, the approved safety report provides additional information. The developer uses the information to define safety distances and monitoring measures;

    b.   Require the developer to submit (to the environmental authority) the screening documentation, including details about safety distances and an analysis of the expected adverse effects resulting from the increased risk and the consequences from a major accident situation from existing hazardous facilities;

    c.   Send the screening information to the competent authorities for opinions on constructions if there are special legislative requirements for safety distances for the facility;

    d.   Issue a screening decision including information on safety distances, any conditions and measures.

The screening decision is publicly accessible and subject to appeal.

Box 3 - Belgium (Flanders Region): integrating industrial accidents safety considerations into land-use planning by means of the strategic environmental assessment process

In the Flanders Region of Belgium, the legal and regulatory framework coordinates SEA and industrial accidents safety considerations under the SEA land-use planning procedures.

The SEA screening verifies the presence of establishments subject to the Seveso III Directive within a 2-kilometre radius of the concerned plan (Seveso test), which is part of the scoping. The SEA needs to incorporate relevant conclusions from the safety report, if available. Public participation is obligatory for each land-use plan. Transboundary consultations take place whenever a transboundary impact is expected.

Consultations with the environmental and safety authorities are a statutory obligation when Seveso III Directive establishments are present. During siting, a number of authorities participate in the SEA and EIA processes, including the initiator or advisory authority (such as Urban Planning Flanders), the EIA/SEA unit for process management and quality control and other authorities with specific environmental responsibilities. Advice is sought by relevant provinces or municipalities.

Box 4 - Portugal: integrating industrial accidents safety considerations into environmental impact assessment and strategic environmental assessment processes

In Portugal, Decree-Law 150/2015 coordinates the industrial accidents safety considerations under the Seveso III Directive with SEA procedures for land-use planning and EIA procedures regarding the siting of hazardous activities.

When new sites or significant changes to existing sites are subject to EIA, the EIA includes a land-use compatibility assessment and information on major accidents. That assessment is included in the environmental report. The competent authority for the Industrial Accidents Convention participates in the assessment commission that evaluates the environmental report, and both decisions are integrated.

Portuguese legislation provides, in the EIA Decree, the minimum procedures for transboundary consultations for projects likely to have significant environmental impacts vis-à-vis another European Union member State. The results of the consultations held in other member States must be transmitted to the national authorities.

A bilateral protocol between Portugal and Spain exists since 2008 to simplify the formalities, allowing direct transmission of documents and data to the national competent authorities, in parallel with the formal communications by the foreign ministries.

In the SEA procedure, and according to the Decree-Law 232/2007, the entities consulted depend on the specific plan and the potential effects of its application. If a land-use plan includes areas where hazardous activities are located, the Portuguese Environment Agency is consulted regarding industrial accidents. In this regard, guidance related to the integration of major accidents prevention in the SEA of land-use municipal plans is available, in Portuguese.

The SEA Decree sets out procedures for carrying out transboundary consultations for plans or programmes likely to have significant environmental transboundary effects. The consultation outcomes are transmitted to the competent national authorities. Portugal also participates in the SEA of other States when their plans and programmes are likely to have significant environmental effects in Portugal. The Portuguese Environment

Agency is consulted for Spanish plans and programmes, and the results are transmitted to the Spanish authorities. The consultations' outcomes are included in the environmental report and the plan or programme.

The legal framework for public participation is in line with the Aarhus Convention and the European Union Directive on SEA.8 The public concerned (i.e., citizens, companies, and environmental non-governmental organizations) is defined on a case-by-case basis, depending on the type of plan or programme and its location. For local or regional plans or programmes, it is mandatory to consult municipalities or the regional coordination body.

Box 5 - United Kingdom of Great Britain and Northern Ireland: consultation with the competent safety authorities during siting of proposed developments near hazardous activities

The Health and Safety Executive (HSE) serves as the competent safety authority in the United Kingdom. It notifies the local planning authorities of the location of hazardous activities. A planning authority then seeks the advice of HSE when considering applications for planning permissions for specific developments in the vicinity of hazardous activities. Consultations with HSE in planning are mandatory in these cases. When consulted by the planning authority regarding an application relating to hazardous substances consent, HSE uses the zones within the area to check compatibility of the consent with existing development in the vicinity.

Box 6 - Estonia: the role of competent safety authorities in decision-making regarding land use

The Estonian Rescue Board (crisis management department and regional and local rescue centres) is responsible for prevention and emergency preparedness for industrial accidents. The Board is actively involved in siting and land-use procedures and related EIA and SEA processes, including screening and scoping, and has a number of binding powers in this respect.

Comprehensive, special or detailed spatial plans and building design documentation must be submitted to the Board for approval when:

    a.   Selecting the location of a new establishment;

    b.   Expanding the operations of an existing establishment or increasing production, provided that a plan needs to be initiated or amended or a building permit needs to be granted;

    c.   Planning an area located in the danger zone of a hazardous enterprise, an enterprise with a major hazard, or planning construction works there.

The Board assesses whether:

    a.   The plan or construction works increase the major-accident hazard or the severity of its consequences;

    b.   The planned accident prevention measures are sufficient;

    c.   The operator of the establishment must submit additional information to the local authority and to the Board before the plan is adopted or the building permit is granted.

The Board may reject a proposal if a planned activity in the plan or in the building design documentation increases the risk of a major accident occurrence, or the severity of its consequences, and the planned accident prevention measures are insufficient.

IV. Guidance on legal, procedural and administrative aspects

46. Guidance is provided below on how to implement obligations under the legal instruments in an integrated manner, with a particular focus on screening, scoping, the environmental report and the flow of information. The guidance is followed by table 2, which outlines relevant provisions of the Protocol on SEA and the Industrial Accidents Convention on land-use planning, siting and modification of hazardous activities and their linkages. It also provides recommended practical advice for integrating the obligations under the two instruments.

A. General obligations and approaches to their implementation

47. The Industrial Accidents Convention requires that Parties develop and implement policies and strategies for reducing the risk of industrial accidents and improving preventive, preparedness and response measures (article 3, para. 2). Parties have to take appropriate legislative, regulatory, administrative and financial measures for the prevention of, preparedness for and response to industrial accidents (article 3, para. 4).

48. In implementing the above general obligations, as well as specific obligations under article 7 of the Industrial Accidents Convention, most Parties seek to ensure that the objectives of preventing industrial accidents and limiting the consequences of such accidents are taken into account in their land-use or other relevant policies and strategies referred to in article 3, paragraph 2, in particular through controls on:

    a. The siting of new hazardous activities;

    b. Significant modifications to existing hazardous activities;

    c. The type and location of new developments, including transport routes and residential and public use areas, which, by virtue of being in the vicinity of a hazardous activity, may increase the risk or consequences of an industrial accident.

49. To be effective, the obligations under the Industrial Accidents Convention, in particular on safety considerations, are recommended to be formally included in land-use planning and siting decisions, alongside the obligations arising from the Espoo Convention and the Protocol on SEA (see chapter II and table 1).

50. This formal inclusion can be achieved, including through the introduction of substantive and procedural obligations into the land-use planning and siting framework.

51. Substantive obligations may be included either in binding normative acts or in soft law instruments such as guidelines or guidance notes. Procedural obligations are typically included in binding normative acts.

52. Reliance only on substantive or only on procedural obligations may not be sufficient. Better results can be achieved when combining substantive and procedural obligations.

53. It is important to ensure the comprehensive and effective flow of information between all stakeholders, including operators of hazardous activities, the public, competent safety authorities, planning authorities and environmental and health authorities. This requires that the appropriate framework be established for the provision of information between the Party of origin and affected Parties and between authorities and the public.

B. Substantive obligations

54. The obligations under the Industrial Accidents Convention related to minimizing the risk to the population and the environment through siting decisions (article 7) are recommended be formally included in land-use decision-

making. This could be achieved through a clear legal requirement that land-use plans, programmes or other relevant policies and strategies, decision-making procedures for implementing those policies and strategies, and specific decisions on siting, take into account, inter alia, the need in the long term to:

    a. Maintain appropriate safety distances between hazardous activities and residential areas, buildings and areas of public use, recreational areas and, as far as possible, major transport routes;

    b. Protect areas of particular natural sensitivity or interest in the vicinity of hazardous activities, where appropriate through adequate safety distances or other relevant measures;

    c. Take additional technical measures necessary for the safe performance of the existing hazardous activity and for the prevention of industrial accidents so as not to increase the risks to human health and the environment.

55. To make the above legal requirements operational, they may be supplemented in the form of either legal requirements or guidance, by referring to matters set out in annex V, paragraph 2, subparagraphs (1) to (8), and annex VI to the Industrial Accidents Convention, which should be considered during the respective decision-making.

56. The above substantive obligations may be included in the respective decision-making in different ways, alongside the obligations arising from the Espoo Convention and the Protocol on SEA, in particular by:

    a. Establishing a clear legal requirement obligating planning authorities to address the above matters in their decisions;

    b. Establishing a clear legal requirement to address the above matters in the respective EIA or SEA procedures;

    c. Combining the two methods set out in (a) and (b) above.

57. In coordinated or combined procedures, the effects covered under the Industrial Accidents Convention can be reported along with the environmental report (either separately or as part of it). These effects are recommended to be at least summarized within the environmental report to allow their systematic consideration within the EIA or SEA process, further to the Espoo Convention and Protocol on SEA, respectively.

58. Reporting the fulfilment of substantive obligations in the statement of reasons and considerations on which the decision has been based represents a standard practice in many countries. Hence, it may be useful to introduce a special requirement to this effect into the respective legal schemes.

C. Procedural obligations

59. Procedural obligations aimed at ensuring that industrial accidents and safety considerations are formally included in land-use decision-making may take different forms, for example by:

    a. Involving competent safety authorities in the decision-making;

    b. Involving competent safety authorities in the respective EIA or SEA procedures;

    c. A combination of the two methods set out in (a) and (b) above.

60. National frameworks where competent safety authorities' involvement is expected in land-use, EIA or SEA procedures often provide only a general reference — "where appropriate" — to ensure their participation, without specifying concrete criteria for determining whether they should be involved. However, there are practical examples of procedural mechanisms that facilitate the identification of situations in which the competent safety authority must be involved.

61. In the SEA or EIA procedures, when specifying which public (environmental and/or health authorities) to consult, the consultation of authorities dealing with safety issues might be considered. Therefore, whenever the nature of a plan or programme subject to SEA or of an activity subject to EIA is assessed, the consultation of safety-related public authorities is recommended.

62. Under the Protocol on SEA, the environmental and health authorities must be consulted during screening (article 5, para. 2), scoping (article 6, para. 2) and on the draft plan or programme and environmental report (article 9, para. 2). A similar good practice approach is taken in several national frameworks where environmental and health authorities are consulted in all the stages of the EIA procedure.

63. In most national frameworks, the procedural involvement of the competent safety authorities, if envisaged, in the land-use decision-making or respective EIA or SEA procedures is of a consultative nature. However, there are examples where their more prominent role further assures the inclusion of safety considerations into the procedures.

D. Screening

64. Screening criteria under the Espoo Convention and the Protocol on SEA include a number of factors where safety aspects of hazardous activities may be of relevance, such as the general reference to risks to the environment (including health) or the degree to which a plan may affect a valuable area (see annex III to the Protocol). Such reference may be overly general and insufficient to address properly the relevance of the hazards of industrial accidents. It may be useful to include in the national EIA scheme the likelihood of an accident among the screening criteria, as in the European Union SEA Directive.

65. The screening procedure may become even more effective if the general reference to the likelihood of an accident is supplemented by more specific criteria, either in the legislation or in guidance notes. These specific criteria should take into account the relevant matters indicated in annexes V and VI to the Industrial Accidents Convention. They may apply both in the case of the siting of hazardous activities and in the case of land-use plans or the siting of any other activities in the vicinity of hazardous activities.

66. Moreover, a reference to the possibility of accidents might benefit from being supplemented by a legal requirement to include relevant information in the screening document that the developer is required to submit for the purpose of screening under the national EIA scheme.

67. The involvement of competent safety authorities in screening might serve as well for properly identifying activities that should be subject to assessment, as a complementary measure assisting them in identifying the hazardous activities.

68. The screening criteria under the Espoo Convention or any national EIA scheme may apply for the purpose of fulfilling the obligations under article 7 of the Industrial Accidents Convention in relation to the determination of the significance for new hazardous activities and significant modifications to existing hazardous activities.

69. In determining whether a proposed plan or programme sets the framework for future development consent of projects listed in annexes I and II to the Protocol on SEA, the hazardous activities listed in annex I to the Industrial Accidents Convention are recommended to be considered as an inclusive element complementing the aforementioned requirements. This consideration can be done in consultation with the competent safety authorities.

E. Scoping and the environmental report

70. Planning authorities need to be provided with relevant information in order to undertake adequate and sufficient consideration of safety issues in their decision-making on land-use plans or programmes or siting. The respective environmental reports provide important sources of information that are provided by the proponent of the plan, programme or project to the authorities, as long as the scope of information has been adequately and sufficiently determined during the scoping phase. In addition, the contingency plans that are prepared by the proponent under the Industrial Accidents Convention are useful sources of information for the authorities.

71. Therefore, proper determination of the scope of assessment in the EIA or SEA procedure is required, and depends on the information provided for the purpose of the plan, programme or project.[8] The Espoo Convention and the Protocol on SEA do not detail what information is to be presented for the purpose of scoping. Many Parties, however, provide clear requirements in this respect in their national legislation.

72. To improve the consideration of safety issues in decision-making, requirements included in some national legislation could be supplemented with one that information regarding safety issues be addressed. Parties are recommended to consider introducing a direct obligation to address safety aspects of hazardous activities in the environmental reports prepared in accordance with the Espoo Convention and the Protocol on SEA.

73. Competent safety authorities should be involved both in scoping and in the review of the environmental reports. For example, the European Union EIA Directive[9] indicates that, where requested by the developer, the competent authority has to issue an opinion on the scope and level of detail of the information to be included by the developer in the environmental report. When determining the scope, the competent authority should take into account information provided by the developer, in particular in relation to the specific characteristics of the project, its location and technical capacity and its likely impact on the environment.

74. Depending on the advice from the scoping consultations with environmental, health and safety authorities, the land-use plan proponent may conduct an EIA or SEA separately, concurrently or jointly with the industrial accidents analysis and evaluation. In any case, it would be useful to have in place arrangements for sharing information generated and for coordinating the recommendations for reducing effects, safe distances and other matters.

F. Flow of information

75. An adequate flow of information is necessary to ensure that land-use decision-making properly considers the objectives of the Industrial Accidents Convention. To achieve this, it is important for Parties to establish procedures that support the flow of information and to agree in advance on the scope of information to be provided in specific cases.

76. Therefore, appropriate mechanisms are recommended to be in place for regular provision of information between competent safety authorities and planning authorities, including contingency plans referred to in article 8 of the Industrial Accidents Convention and the information received pursuant transboundary consultations under article 4 of that Convention. Such mechanisms may be independent from the appropriate consultation procedures required by the Protocol on SEA and the Espoo and Aarhus Conventions.

77. For land-use planning purposes under SEA procedures, it is necessary to have all information available for comment by the public, the relevant environmental and health authorities and the competent safety authorities. The information must include the proposed plan or programme and the accompanying environmental report, and could usefully be supplemented by relevant information from the analysis and evaluation of hazardous activities under annex V to the Industrial Accidents Convention.

78. Furthermore, Parties are recommended to use a coordinated procedure (if not a single one) for soliciting feedback. The decision-making on the proposed plan or programme is recommended to address outcomes of any analyses and consultations conducted under the Industrial Accidents Convention along with the environmental report and outcomes of consultations under the Protocol on SEA.

---

8 For example, the Parties to the Protocol on SEA decided to develop a *Simplified Resource Manual to Support Application of the Protocol on Strategic Environmental Assessment* (ECE/MP.EIA/18), which suggests that the objectives of the plan or programme, relevant environmental problems and more general environmental objectives can support the determination of the scope of an SEA environmental report.

9 Directive 2011/92/EU of the European Parliament and of the Council of 13 December 2011 on the assessment of the effects of certain public and private projects on the environment, as amended by Directive 2014/52/EU of the European Parliament and of the Council of 16 April 2014.

79. In relation to siting decisions, the EIA procedures are recommended to be designed to ensure that operators provide sufficient risk information about the hazardous activity and make available technical advice on those risks, either case by case or on a generic basis, when decisions are taken. Parties are recommended to also strive to ensure that the procedures are coordinated and that the relevant authorities consult each other on risk information.

80. Coordinated procedures under the relevant instruments require that the information on an adopted plan, programme or project be presented to the public in a coordinated way. When producing a statement of reasons and considerations on which a land-use planning or siting decision has been based, all the information requirements of the relevant instruments (Industrial Accidents Convention, article 9, para. 1; Protocol on SEA, article 11, para. 2; Espoo Convention, article 6, para. 2) should be satisfied.

81. For industrial safety planning, SEA and EIA procedures, the quality of the documentation used during the public participation process, in particular screening and scoping documents and environmental reports, depends on the information available. As preparers of the respective documentation, usually private consultants, rely mostly on publicly available information, proper arrangements are recommended to be made to ensure that information, in particular that referred to in annex VIII to the Industrial Accidents Convention, is permanently available to the public, including in electronic databases that are easily accessible through public telecommunications networks. The information is recommended to be periodically reviewed and, where necessary, updated, including in the event of significant modifications to hazardous activities.

82. Regarding information that is confidential (for example, for security reasons) or commercially sensitive and therefore not publicly available, the proponent preparing an SEA or EIA report is recommended to request the information from the relevant authorities. The authorities should be obliged to provide the information upon reasonable request.

Table 2 - Overview of the relevant provisions of the Protocol on Strategic Environmental Assessment and the Industrial Accidents Convention on land-use planning, siting and modification of hazardous activities and their linkages

Provisions with logical linkages	Protocol on SEA	Industrial Accidents Convention	Recommendations
Application to plans	Art. 4, para. 3: "[An SEA] shall be carried out for plans and programmes which are prepared for [mentioned sectors] and which set the framework for future development consent for projects listed in annex I and any other project listed in annex II that requires an [EIA] under national legislation".	Art. 7: "the Party of origin shall … seek the establishment of policies on the siting of new hazardous activities and on significant modifications to existing hazardous activities" and "on significant developments in areas which could be affected by transboundary effects of an industrial accident … [The] Parties should consider the matters set out in annex V, paragraph 2, subparagraphs (1) to (8), and annex VI hereto".	The SEA process is recommended to consider whether the proposed land-use plan influences or takes into account the hazardous activities addressed under the Industrial Accidents Convention. This can be done by consulting the nationally designated authorities for implementation of the Industrial Accidents Convention.

Provisions with logical linkages	Protocol on SEA	Industrial Accidents Convention	Recommendations
Projects set in the framework of plans and programmes (Protocol on SEA) "Hazardous activities" (Industrial Accidents Convention)	Art. 4, para. 3: "projects listed in annex I and any other project listed in annex II that requires an [EIA] under national legislation".	Art. 1 (b): "Hazardous activity" means "any activity in which one or more hazardous substances are present or may be present in quantities at or in excess of the threshold quantities listed in annex I hereto, and which is capable of causing transboundary effects".	The SEA screening can be required to specify whether the proposed plan or programme addresses land use related to existing or proposed installations for hazardous substances. This can be done by consulting the nationally designated authorities for implementation of the Industrial Accidents Convention. Detailed information about new proposed "hazardous activities" might not be available in the SEA process, but such early consultations can nevertheless specify whether the proposed land use influences or takes account of the existing or proposed installations where industrial accidents can happen.
"Environmental, including health, effect" (Protocol on SEA) "Effects" resulting from an "Industrial accident" (Industrial Accidents Convention)	Art. 2, para. 7: "Environmental, including health, effect" means "any effect on the environment, including human health, flora, fauna, biodiversity, soil, climate, air, water, landscape, natural sites, material assets, cultural heritage and the interaction among these factors". Annex IV, footnote to item 6: "These effects should include secondary, cumulative, synergistic, short-, medium- and long-term, permanent and temporary, positive and negative effects".	Art. 1, subpara. (c): "Effects" means "any direct or indirect, immediate or delayed adverse consequences…on: (i) Human beings, flora and fauna; (ii) Soil, water, air and landscape; (iii) The interaction between the factors in (i) and (ii)". Art. 1, subpara. (a): "Industrial accident" is "an event resulting from an uncontrolled development … involving hazardous substances either: (i) In an installation … or (ii) During transportation".	Effects caused by industrial accidents under the Industrial Accidents Convention can be considered as a subset of environmental, including health, effects under the Protocol on SEA.

Provisions with logical linkages	Protocol on SEA	Industrial Accidents Convention	Recommendations
Determination of the scope of the assessment (Protocol on SEA) Analysis and evaluation (Industrial Accidents Convention)	Art. 6, para. 1: "Each Party shall establish arrangements for the determination of the relevant information to be included in the environmental report". Art. 6, para. 2: "Each Party shall ensure that the environmental and health authorities … are consulted when determining the relevant information to be included in the environmental report".	Art. 6, para. 2: "the Party of origin shall require the operator to demonstrate the safe performance of the hazardous activity by the provision of information … including but not limited to, analysis and evaluation". Annex V, item 1: "The analysis and evaluation of the hazardous activity should be performed with a scope and to a depth which vary depending on the purpose for which they are carried out."	For an SEA of a proposed land-use plan, the nationally designated authorities for implementation of the Industrial Accidents Convention are recommended to be consulted to determine what kind of information (including the level of detail) from annex V should be provided in the environmental report in the SEA process to maximize the linkages and reduce overlaps.
Environmental report (Protocol on SEA) Analysis and evaluation (Industrial Accidents Convention)	Annex IV (content of the environmental report): "1. The contents and the main objectives of the plan or programme and its link with other plans or programmes. 2. The relevant aspects of the current state of the environment …; 3. The characteristics of the environment …; 4. The environmental, including health, problems …; 5. The environmental, including health, objectives established at international, national and other levels …; 6. The likely significant environmental, including health, effects. 7. Measures to prevent, reduce or mitigate any significant adverse effects …;	Annex V (Analysis and evaluation): "(1) The quantities and properties of hazardous substances on the site; (2) Brief descriptive scenarios … of industrial accidents possibly arising from the hazardous activity … (3) For each scenario: (a) The approximate quantity of a release; (b) The extent and severity of the resulting consequences … in favourable and unfavourable conditions …; (c) The time-scale within which the industrial accident could develop … (d) Any action which could be taken to minimize the likelihood of escalation; (4) The size and distribution of the population in the vicinity …; (5) The age, mobility and susceptibility of that population; (6) The severity of the harm inflicted on people and the environment …; (7) The distance from the location of the hazardous activity at which harmful effects on people and the environment may reasonably occur …;	Depending on the advice from scoping consultations, the proponent of the land-use plan may conduct SEA and analysis and evaluation of industrial accidents separately, concurrently or jointly. Nevertheless, arrangements are recommended to be made for sharing information generated and the recommendations for reducing the effects, safe distances, etc., are recommended to be coordinated.

Provisions with logical linkages	Protocol on SEA	Industrial Accidents Convention	Recommendations
Environmental report (Protocol on SEA) *Analysis and evaluation (Industrial Accidents Convention)* *(Continued)*	8. An outline of the reasons for selecting the alternatives dealt with and a description of how the assessment was undertaken …; 9. Measures envisaged for monitoring …; 10. The likely significant transboundary environmental, including health, effects. 11. A non-technical summary of the information provided."	(8) The same information … for planned or reasonably foreseeable future developments; (9) The people who may be affected by an industrial accident."	
Public participation	Art. 8, para. 2: "Each Party … shall ensure the timely public availability of the draft plan or programme and the environmental report." Art. 8, para. 4: "Each Party shall ensure that the public has the opportunity to express its opinion … within a reasonable time frame." Art. 8, para. 5: "Each Party shall ensure that the detailed arrangements for informing the public and consulting the public concerned are determined and made publicly available…"	Art. 9, para. 2: "The Party of origin shall … give the public … an opportunity to participate in relevant procedures … and shall ensure that the opportunity given to the public of the affected Party is equivalent to that given to the public of the Party of origin." Annex III, item 9: "The Parties concerned shall inform the public in areas reasonably capable of being affected …, arrange for the distribution of the analysis and evaluation documentation to it and to the authorities … [and] ensure them an opportunity for making comments on, or objections to, the hazardous activity".	All information (the proposed land-use plan, the environmental report and the analysis and evaluation) should be available for public comments. There may also be a coordinated procedure for soliciting public feedback. This could be based on annex V to the SEA Protocol and annex VIII to the Industrial Accidents Convention.
Consultations with relevant authorities	Art. 9, para. 2: "The draft plan or programme and the environmental report shall be made available to the environmental and health authorities." Art. 9, para. 3. "Each Party shall ensure that environmental and health authorities are given … the opportunity to express their opinion".	See above. Annex III, item 9 provides for consultations with both the public and authorities in the relevant areas.	The proposed land-use plan, environmental report and the analysis and evaluation can be made available for comments by the relevant authorities.

Provisions with logical linkages	Protocol on SEA	Industrial Accidents Convention	Recommendations
Decision-making	Art. 11, para. 1: "Each Party shall ensure that … due account is taken of: (a) The conclusions of the environmental report; (b) The measures to prevent, reduce or mitigate the adverse effects…; and (c) The comments received".	Annex VI: "The following illustrates the matters which should be considered [in decision-making on siting]: 1. The results of risk analysis and evaluation …; 2. The results of consultations and public participation processes; 3. An analysis of the increase or decrease of the risk …; 4. The evaluation of environmental risks …; 5. An evaluation of the new hazardous activities …; 6. A consideration of the siting of new, and significant modifications to existing hazardous activities …, as well as the establishment of a safety area around hazardous activities".	Decision-making on the proposed plan or programme is recommended to address outcomes of any analyses and consultations conducted under the Industrial Accidents Convention along with the environmental report and outcomes of consultations under the Protocol.
Information on decision	Art. 11, para. 2: "Each Party shall ensure that, when a plan or programme is adopted, the public, the relevant environmental and health authorities and the Parties … are informed, and that the plan or programme is made available".	Art. 9, para. 1: "The Parties shall ensure that adequate information is given to the public in the areas capable of being affected by an industrial accident" and "shall include the elements in annex VIII". Annex VIII: "1. The name of the company, address of the hazardous activity and identification by position held of the person giving the information; 2. An explanation in simple terms of the hazardous activity …; 3. The common names or the generic names or the general danger classification of the substances and preparations …; 4. General information resulting from an environmental impact assessment …; 5. The general information relating to the nature of an industrial accident …, including its potential effects …;	Information on the decision (i.e., the adopted land-use plan) is recommended to be provided jointly or in a coordinated manner, in order to reduce overlap between the information provided under the Protocol (article 11, para. 2), and the Industrial Accidents Convention (article 9, para. 1).

Provisions with logical linkages	Protocol on SEA	Industrial Accidents Convention	Recommendations
Information on decision *(Continued)*		6. Adequate information on how the affected population will be warned and kept informed …; 7. Adequate information on the actions the affected population should take …; 8. Adequate information on arrangements made …, including liaison with the emergency services …; 9. General information on the emergency services' off-site contingency plan …; 10. General information on special requirements and conditions … , including licensing or authorization systems; 11. Details of where further relevant information can be obtained."	

Part B
Technical Guidance on Land-Use Planning,
the Siting of Hazardous Activities
and related Safety Aspects

I. Introduction

A. Objective

1. The present technical guidance aims to support the implementation of the Convention on the Transboundary Effects of Industrial Accidents (Industrial Accidents Convention) in relation to land-use planning, siting and related safety aspects of hazardous activities, with a focus on the risk aspects of hazardous facilities. It supplements the general guidance (Part A).

B. Framework of the Industrial Accidents Convention and safety guidelines

2. The Industrial Accidents Convention and the following UNECE safety guidelines set the framework for the present technical guidance by providing provisions to assist countries in preventing the occurrence of industrial accidents, mitigating or minimizing their impacts, and promoting active international cooperation between countries before, during and after an accident:

    a. *The Safety Guidelines and Good Practices for Tailings Management Facilities*[1] address the need for land-use planning considerations to be taken into account when evaluating optimum siting of tailings management facilities, and the need to carry out an environmental impact assessment prior to construction as well as a risk assessment;

    b. *The Safety Guidelines and Good Industry Practices for Oil Terminals*[2] recognize that siting and land-use planning can have significant effects on oil terminal hazards and identify the need for risk assessment. For new oil terminals, the competent authorities must take into account appropriate safety distances from transport routes and the locations of public-use and residential areas and areas of natural sensitivity or interest;

    c. *The Safety Guidelines and Good Practices for Pipelines*[3] suggest that land-use planning considerations should be taken into account both in route planning for new pipelines and in decisions concerning proposals for new developments near existing pipelines. An annex is dedicated to risk assessment and land-use planning.

3. The *Guidelines to Facilitate the Identification of Hazardous Activities for the Purposes of the Convention*[4] provide two location criteria for the purpose of identifying hazardous activities capable of causing transboundary effects under the Convention:

    a. Within 15 kilometres from the border, for activities involving substances that may cause a fire or explosion or involving toxic substances that may be released into the air in the event of an accident;

    b. Along or within the catchment areas of transboundary and border rivers, transboundary or international lakes, or within the catchment areas of transboundary groundwaters, for activities involving toxic or extremely flammable substances or substances that are very toxic to aquatic organisms.

---

1 ECE/CP.TEIA/26, available from http://www.unece.org/index.php?id=36132.

2 ECE/CP.TEIA/28, available from http://www.unece.org/index.php?id=41066.

3 ECE/CP.TEIA/27, available from http://www.unece.org/index.php?id=41068.

4 See decision 2000/3 (ECE/CP.TEIA/2, annex IV, appendix), as amended by decision 2004/2 (ECE/CP.TEIA/12, annex II), both available from http://www.unece.org/env/teia/guidelines.html.

II. Technical guidance on planning and risk assessment methods

A. Introduction to land-use planning

4.   There are several formal definitions of land-use planning but all of them have a common understanding that it is a process by which land is allocated and regulated for different socioeconomic activities such as agriculture, housing, industry, recreation and commerce, in order to manage the siting of activities and prevent land-use conflicts. Hence, land-use planning decisions must account for all sources of risk, both natural and man-made, which include potential threats to human health, property and the environment arising from hazardous facilities (both existing and proposed new facilities).

5.   The technical, administrative and legislative processes for making decisions on the siting and type of activities, including hazardous activities, should be consistent with applicable national laws, regulations, policies and legislation or international agreements.

6.   This chapter describes the methods for land-use planning and risk assessment close to hazardous facilities, with consideration of transboundary effects. It should be noted that emissions of hazardous substances into water bodies have been responsible for the vast majority of transboundary accidents to date and therefore drainage, flooding and other hydrological matters around hazardous activities should be given particular attention. The following land-use planning approaches should be considered as illustrative and not as recommendations by UNECE. The approaches may have changed since this guidance was issued.

7.   National urban planning policies and frameworks must take into consideration new legislation (e.g., the European Union Seveso III Directive)[5] to explicitly address the risks posed by existing or future hazardous activities.

B. Land-use planning and risk assessment approaches

8.   The UNECE countries rely on technical and scientific information to support their land-use planning decision-making, a part of which is based upon the risk assessment methodology and risk acceptance criteria. The land-use planning approaches can be grouped under four categories:

   a.   **Deterministic approach:** defines generic distances which are determined by the kind of hazardous activity considered, operational acquired experience, environmental impact and expert judgment;

   b.   **Consequence-based approach:** identifies worst-case potential consequences and evaluates the effects (e.g., fatalities and injuries to individuals);

   c.   **Risk-based approach:** assesses both the consequences and frequency of the accident occurrence to evaluate the individual and/or societal risk;

   d.   **Semi-quantitative (or semi-probabilistic) approach:** a method based on a quantitative evaluation of the consequence and a qualitative estimation of its occurrence frequency.

   Hybrid approaches combining two or more of the methods above are also used.

---

5   Directive 2012/18/EU of the European Parliament and of the Council of 4 July 2012 on the control of major-accident hazards involving dangerous substances, amending and subsequently repealing Council Directive 96/82/EC.

9. The deterministic approach is a straightforward method that relies on expert judgment in defining generic distances between areas designated for hazardous activities and areas designated for residential, public or other community purposes. Predefined generic distances are set for different types of hazardous activities, based upon the types of hazardous substances and activities present at the facility, historical data and previous accidents occurring at similar facilities. Hence, these distances are not related to risk or based on a detailed analysis of the facility. Under this approach, a gradual land-use plan should be developed whereby incompatible activities (such as industrial and residential areas) are located at a specified minimum distance from each other.

10. The consequence-based approach focuses on the assessment of the most significant potential impacts arising from accidents, including thermal radiation, overpressure and toxic concentration effects. It does not involve an evaluation of the frequency of occurrence of accidents. Damage threshold values for these consequences are determined (examples are given in table 1). Based on the damage threshold values, distances can be specified and mapped, showing different levels of consequences. An illustrative example of five threshold values for chlorine continuous release is provided in figure 1. Based on these thresholds, urban planners can stipulate the areas where certain activities, such as residential use, are forbidden (i.e., within the red zone) and where they may be considered (i.e., within the dark blue zone). Such an approach was used in France before the disaster at Toulouse in 2001 and is being used in other countries.

11. The risk-based approach uses a quantitative risk assessment method to calculate both the consequences of the identified accident scenario and its expected frequency of occurrence. The analysis is performed for a set of accident scenarios and requires large amounts of data, such as components failure frequency data, effect endpoints values and population and environmental data, as well as models for calculating the consequences and effects. The two risk measures that are usually calculated are individual risk and societal risk, which are represented respectively under the form of risk contours, societal risk curves and societal risk maps. The Netherlands evaluates land-use compatibility through societal risk and societal risk maps, the latter being easier for the public to understand.

Table 1 - Examples of types of damage thresholds for determining distances

Consequence	Effect-Distance
Thermal effects	Determination of a distance corresponding to a thermal radiation which, for a given exposure period, can cause burns likely to be lethal or cause serious injury
Explosion	Determination of a distance corresponding to an overpressure likely to be lethal or cause serious injury (e.g., burst eardrums)
Toxic release	Determination of a distance corresponding to a lethal toxic dose or serious injury

Figure 1 - Example of chlorine continuous release

Source: Major Accident Hazards Bureau of the European Commission's Joint Research Centre.

Note: Figure shows release as modelled by ADAM 1.0 and against a backdrop provided by Google Earth.

12. The semi-quantitative approach uses a hybrid method based on a quantitative evaluation of the consequence of an accident and a qualitative estimation of its frequency of occurrence. The worst-case accident scenario is generally selected. The assessment needs data such as effect endpoint values, population and environmental data and models for calculating the consequences and effects. The outcomes of the consequence assessment can be presented as damage thresholds values. The frequency of accidents is represented under four to five classes. Then the consequences and frequencies are presented on a risk map, representing different levels of risk. This approach is used in France and Italy.

13. The environmental risk assessment of an accident and its potential effects on fauna and flora is more qualitative in nature compared to the approaches used for human risk. There are a lack of mature (and standard) mathematical models to estimate the effects on fauna and flora, making the identification of acceptable environmental risk levels or criteria inherently difficult. The qualitative approaches focus on hazard identification and assessing prevention and control measures. Belgium (Flanders Region), Ireland, Italy, Spain and the United Kingdom of Great Britain and Northern Ireland use these approaches, whereby their authorities determine whether sufficient measures have been taken by the facility or operator to prevent, protect and minimize accidents and their effects on the environment.

C. Key steps in land-use planning procedures

14. This section provides guidance on mapping and the key steps that Parties[6] should adopt in their land-use planning and risk assessment procedural frameworks for:

    a. Decisions on new land-use policies, plans or programmes. The major challenge is determining and managing the compatibility of hazardous activities or land uses with surrounding land uses;

    b. Decisions on siting of new hazardous facilities (projects). The challenge is determining and managing the risk and effects associated with the siting of a new hazardous facility;

    c. Decisions on significant modifications to existing hazardous facilities (projects). The challenge is determining and managing the increased risk and effects of an existing hazardous facility owing to modifications to the facility's buildings, hazardous substances, activities, etc.;

    d. Decisions on new developments near existing hazardous facilities (projects). The challenge is determining and managing the increased risk and effects of an existing hazardous facility owing to a new development (e.g., residential) near an existing facility.

1. Important land-use and risk mapping considerations

15. Decision-making on land-use policies, plans, programmes and projects should take into consideration how the risks to health, environment and property can be minimized in the event of an accident involving hazardous substances, in order to determine whether to approve or refuse the proposal.

16. Mapping is a necessary part of planning, to illustrate clearly the existing environmental conditions, the location of urban areas, land uses, potential risk sources and potential effects. For land-use planning and risk assessment in relation to hazardous activities, a set of maps should be produced that describe the area and show the location of:

    a. Existing land uses in areas surrounding the hazardous activity (e.g., residential (high-density, medium and low-density areas), industrial, commercial, public and agricultural);

    b. Existing urban development (e.g., buildings and infrastructure), transport networks and local population;

    c. Existing environmental features and hydrogeology (e.g., topography, vegetation, surface water and groundwater);

---

6   Parties to the Industrial Accidents Convention, the Protocol on SEA and/or the Espoo Convention.

d. Areas of interest (e.g., forest, recreational spaces and coasts);

e. Sensitive and protected areas (e.g., national parks, protected habitats and cultural heritage);

f. Vulnerable people (e.g., in hospitals, old people's homes, schools and parks) or where high numbers of people may be present at one time (e.g., churches, shopping centres, theatres and railway stations);

g. Existing industrial risk sources, considering both facilities and transport of hazardous substances;

h. Other potential risk sources, such as transport of hazardous substances and natural disasters (flooding, earthquakes and domino effects);

i. Proposed hazardous facilities and activities, including the boundaries, dimensions, infrastructure, buildings, substances, utilities, workforce and off-site transport;

j. Potential off-site effects of proposed hazardous activities;

k. The location and availability of external emergency response capability (fire brigades, hospitals, etc.).

17. The above set of maps should be overlaid to evaluate the compatibility of hazardous activities with the land uses around them. By using modern risk assessment tools (based on geographical information systems), all georeferenced maps and spatial risk data can be overlapped to clearly present the data. The result is a new land-use map and risk map in which the compatibility of hazardous activities with other land uses and developments can be evaluated.

18. The above mapping procedures should be incorporated into national land-use planning policies, plans, programmes and projects.

2. Considerations for off-site transport corridors

19. Determining and managing land-use compatibility near transport corridors and the risks and effects of transporting hazardous substances (by road, rail, pipeline and waterway) within the land areas crossed are major challenges. It requires different methods of evaluation and control as the risk source moves between land-use zones. It is important to note that the Industrial Accidents Convention only covers transportation on the site of the hazardous activities (article 2, para. 2 (d) (ii)).

20. Emergency management plans should be established, detailing preparation and response measures that aim to minimize the risk of adverse effects on people, property and the environment along the route. In the case of pipelines, the planning controls are similar to those applied to fixed hazardous facilities.[7]

3. Seven key steps to adopt into national land-use planning procedures

21. This subsection provides seven key steps for making land-use and siting decisions, which countries should adopt in their national procedural frameworks.

Step 1: Analysis of the site and the surrounding area

22. A crucial first step in planning procedures is identifying and assessing the existing conditions (the natural elements, climate, buildings, infrastructure and other features) of the area, without the proposed land use or project. This will help to determine the changes or impacts of the proposal and whether it is compatible with the site and surrounding area.

23. This type of information is elaborated and periodically updated by experts or planners and should be available for use at the local municipality. It comprises a set of thematic maps (in digital or paper form), which describe the land use and land conditions before the development of the new land use or new or modified hazardous activity.

---

7   See *Safety Guidelines and Good Practices for Pipelines*.

Step 2: Review of the relevant laws and legislation

24. The next step is to review the existing laws and legislation that are relevant to and will influence the parameters of the proposal, such as the siting of hazardous facilities, the different types of activities permitted or not permitted and environmental laws to be followed.

25. For example, some national legislation establishes the criteria under which a modification should be considered as significant and requiring a permit. For instance, the United Kingdom's Health and Safety Executive (HSE) provides criteria for determining whether modifications could have significant repercussions on the levels of risk to people and the environment.

26. This step also includes a review of the current land-use policies and plans (if present) that designate which types of land use are allowed on the site and the surrounding land. Under some national legislation, these land-use policies and plans (i.e., zoning) stipulate controls such as:

    a.   A set of minimum performance requirements that apply (i.e., to any hazardous activity);

    b.   A mechanism for distinguishing between the types of activities (e.g., low-risk hazardous facilities that are permitted activities, or higher risk facilities that require consent from authorities and may be subject to further controls).

Step 3: Review of documentation about the proposal or land use and the hazardous risk sources

27. It is important to review the documentation available regarding the operation of the proposed development (the new land use, proposed hazardous facility, or new development near existing hazardous activities). These types of documents, for example, planning application reports, land-use plans, safety reports and other expert material, are generally required by regulations, for example by the Seveso III Directive in the European Union.

28. For example, the operator of a proposed facility must inform the relevant authority about the planned activities or modifications and, if considered significant, has to submit a safety report. A safety report must demonstrate that necessary and sufficient measures have been taken to prevent accidents from occurring and, should they occur, to limit their consequences to the population, environment and property.

29. A hazardous facility description may cover:

    a.   The site;

    b.   Meteorological data;

    c.   Main activity and production;

    d.   Organigram and personnel;

    e.   The safety management system;

    f.   Facility perimeters, layout, access routes and protection against intrusion;

    g.   Location of hazardous substances;

    h.   Processing units, storage facilities and waste treatment;

    i.   Substances data (chemical, physical and toxicological properties);

    j.   Monitoring networks (toxic, flammable) and alarms;

    k.   Information made available to the public;

    l.   Activities and safety measures on-site;

    m.   Adopted analysis procedures, models and software tools;

    n.   Hazard identification and accident database consultation;

    o.   Investigation of facility behaviour in case of loss of utilities and external events;

    p.   Accident scenarios based on clear selection criteria;

    q.   Potential consequences of selected scenarios;

r.   Estimation of accident frequency;

s.   Prevention and mitigation measures for each scenario;

t.   Individual and societal risk measures;

u.   Internal emergency plan.

Step 4: Select a planning approach or risk assessment method

30. There are different approaches to land-use planning and risk assessment but they all aim to verify whether the level of risk associated with the proposal is acceptable near a hazardous facility.

31. Land-use approaches and risk assessment methods are described in section II.B. Different approaches can be selected to assess the proposal, based on the risk contours or risk maps produced, or a hybrid approach (combining two of more of the methods) can be applied. National authorities should choose the approach that is most appropriate for dealing with land-use planning and siting of hazardous facilities within their country and for neighbouring countries in the case of potential transboundary effects.

Step 5: Evaluate the potential risks, effects and the compatibility of the hazardous activity

32. Using the planning approaches and risk assessment methods in step 4, the compatibility and risk acceptability of the proposed land use or development with the surrounding area and its potential effects on the population, environment and property can be evaluated.

33. First, a set of criteria must be developed, which the results of the risk assessment are compared against, in order to determine whether the proposal is compatible with surrounding land uses or acceptable in terms of the level of risk and potential effects on the surrounding area.

34. The criteria are created taking into consideration:

a.   The site and context analyses (including the identification of land uses, development and important natural features);

b.   A description of the proposal (including the land-use plans, siting, hazardous activities and measures);

c.   The land-use planning and risk assessment approach (e.g., deterministic, consequence, risk or semi-quantitative based);

d.   An accident risk map showing the land uses, zoning and/or development.

35. In order to describe and illustrate the level of risk, the potential risks posed by the proposal are overlaid on an existing risk map (described in subsection II.C.1). An analysis of the new situation (using the criteria) allows authorities and stakeholders to examine and draw conclusions about the risks, compatibility with surrounding land uses and development and whether decision makers should approve or refuse the proposal.

36. Sophisticated risk quantification software tools are available to evaluate the potential effects of a hazardous activity. For less complex methods of evaluation, the consequence approach can be used, which includes the selection of endpoint values for the different consequences, such as four kilowatts per square metre for thermal radiation. This example represents the fatalities threshold and can be compared with the compatibility criteria. Examples of compatibility are the absence of light industrial buildings, warehouses or two-storey offices within 100 metres of a hazardous facility, low-density housing or hotels within 200 metres and schools, hospitals or care homes within 300 metres. If the hazardous facility is a liquid petroleum gas storage facility, then 100 metres could be added to each distance.

37. When the area of interest for the analysis is described in digital maps, the risk assessment and evaluation of effects can be undertaken using geographical information system-based software tools. For example, the hazardous facility can be represented using different digital maps describing the facility's spatial elements (e.g., building boundaries, layout, location of hazardous substances, utilities, points where accidents may occur and the possible extent of accident effects and/or individual risk contours). A georeferenced grid of a defined cell

dimension is then overlaid on all maps. With all data in digital form, each cell can then be assessed in terms of the effects of accidents (or individual risk value) and compared with the compatibility criteria. This provides, as a result, the areas of incompatibility that require further consideration.

38. For example, a risk assessment for the siting of a hazardous facility includes the following key elements:

    a. Assessment of the types of potential accidents that can lead to the release of hazardous substances;

    b. Estimation of the location, size, rate and duration of the releases;

    c. Determination of the probability of occurrence of the identified type of releases;

    d. Determination of the consequences of each type of release in terms of specific hazard criteria or exposure of people, environment and property;

    e. Comparison of the calculated risk with the risk acceptability criteria.

39. The above risk assessments are more complex when evaluating land-use policies, plans and programmes, as specific projects are not proposed at this stage. These proposals may include national land-use plans that designate areas of land within the country for industrial activities to occur, such as industrial land-use zones. However, general high-level risk assessments and evaluations can be undertaken for these proposals, such as evaluating the distances between, for example, zones for industrial purposes and zones for residential purposes.

For areas that could be affected by industrial accidents of a transboundary nature

40. Past accidents have shown how the off-site effects of an accident at a hazardous facility in one country can have disastrous effects in neighbouring countries. Well known past accidents are those that occurred in Switzerland (1986) and Romania (2000). On 1 November 1986, a major environmental disaster began with a fire at an agrochemical storehouse in Schweizerhalle, Switzerland. Fire brigades sprayed millions of litres of water to extinguish the fire, but the volume of water was too great for existing bunds. Consequently, much of the firewater, mixed with insecticides and other chemicals, entered the Rhine through the Sandoz sewer system.[8] On 30 January 2000, a tailings dam overflowed at the Aurul Mine in Romania and released 100,000 cubic metres of effluent containing cyanide into the Tisza River, which reached the Danube River. A very low level of cyanide was still detected in the river water when it eventually reached the Black Sea.[9]

41. Figure 2 shows the 2,295 facilities subject to the Seveso III Directive that in 2015 were within 5 kilometres of a national border or coastline, of the 10,340 facilities in total. This distance is well within the 15-kilometre proximity criterion under the Industrial Accidents Convention, though the Convention applies broadly to the more significant, upper-tier Seveso facilities, not the smaller, lower-tier ones.

---

[8] France, Ministry of the Environment, "The Rhine polluted by pesticides" (DPPR/SEI/BARPI, No. 5187, October 2006). Available from http://www.aria.developpement-durable.gouv.fr/wp-content/files_mf/FD_5187_schwizerhalle_1986_ang.pdf.

[9] United Nations Environment Programme and Office for the Coordination of Humanitarian Affairs, "Cyanide Spill At Baia Mare Romania: Spill Of Liquid And Suspended Waste At the Aurul S.A. Retreatment Plant in Baia Mare" report of the assessment mission, 23 February–6 March 2000 (Geneva, March 2000). Available from http://reliefweb.int/report/hungary/cyanide-spill-baia-mare-romania-unepocha-assessment-mission-advance-copy.

Figure 2 - Seveso facilities located within 5 kilometres of national borders or coasts

Source: Seveso Plant Information Retrieval System, European Commission Joint Research Centre Major Accident Hazards Bureau.

Notes: A total of 225 facilities (in blue) are close to national borders within the region comprising the European Union and the European Free Trade Association; 71 (in red) are on borders between that region and other States; and the remainder (in green) are in coastal areas.

42. When hazardous activities are capable of causing transboundary effects, the provisions of the Industrial Accidents Convention should be followed. In this case, the above risk assessment and evaluation procedures are still applicable, provided that the concerned countries agree on common approaches for both risk assessment and compatibility criteria.

43. Figure 3 represents a case where a hazardous facility, located in country A, could have effects on the border area in country B. The situation is compounded when hazardous facilities exist on both sides of the border, in countries A and B, as shown in figure 4. In this case, on each side of the border there are two areas that can be differentiated based on the level of impact. For example, in country A the zones that are exposed to the potential effects of an accident occurring in both countries A and B are marked with "Impact B2".

Figure 3 - Transboundary effect of an accident at a hazardous facility located in country A, which may have effects on country B

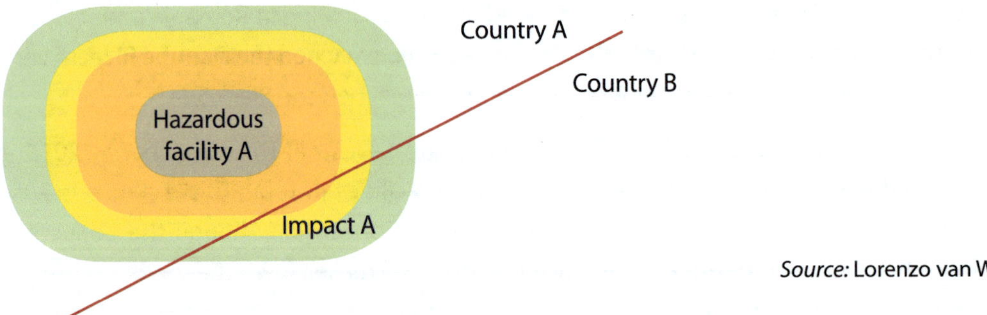

Source: Lorenzo van Wijk.

Figure 4 - Transboundary effects due to the presence of hazardous facilities located in each country and which may have effects on the other country

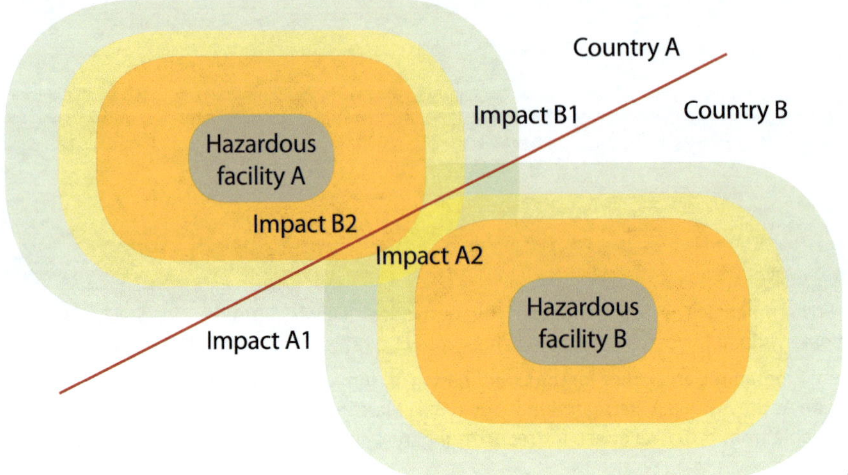

Source: Lorenzo van Wijk.

44. It is important that both countries apply the same risk assessment approach, accident consequence models, frequency estimation methods, environmental data, components reliability data and the compatibility criteria. This enables countries to fulfil the provisions of the Convention and integrate effectively land-use policies, plans, programmes or projects. Unfortunately, this is not often the case.

45. These land-use situations are complex to resolve as they require a strong collaboration between the involved countries and full agreement on the issues above. For this purpose, each country should have full access to all details and safety reports for the relevant hazardous facilities in the adjacent country.

46. Once agreement on methods and models has been achieved, data on the release of hazardous substances (e.g., the release conditions, wind rose and stability classes, consequence models, vulnerability and population distribution) must be collected and shared. Then, the risk assessment for both countries can be repeated with common models and data. As already mentioned, the risk model can be rapidly recalculated if suitable geographic information system-based tools are available.

47. Following this stage, each country can apply its own compatibility criteria to the proposal.

Step 6: International cooperation and public participation

48. Neighbouring countries should exchange information and consult each other to prevent accidents capable of causing transboundary damage and mitigate effects in case they do occur. The country with the existing or planned hazardous activity should provide the relevant information about the activity to all potentially affected countries. The potentially affected countries should provide the country where the activity is located with all relevant information about the area potentially affected. The public in areas capable of being affected should be given the opportunity to participate in land-use planning, siting and licensing procedures for hazardous activities.

49. The above actions should be undertaken in accordance with the Convention.

Step 7: Decisions

50. The previous steps will assist the relevant authorities in making a final decision to approve, refuse, or conditionally approve (subject to changes to the proposal or the stipulation of conditions that must be met):

    a. The proposed land use (land-use policies, plans or programmes);

    b. The proposed project (new hazardous facilities, modifications to existing facilities, or developments in the vicinity of hazardous facilities).

51. Decision makers and stakeholders will need to determine whether these new land uses or developments should be allowed, taking into account the results of the risk assessment and mapping completed in the previous steps.

52. In relation to siting decisions, the project proposal should be permitted when the risk posed by the hazardous activity is below the acceptable threshold and should not be permitted if the calculated risk is above the maximum threshold. However, between the upper and lower acceptability thresholds, the risk is in a grey area where safety improvement and additional mitigation measures may be enforced on the hazardous facility to reduce the risk to the population.

53. In relation to land-use decisions, new land uses in a land-use policy, plan or programme proposal must be compatible with surrounding land uses, taking into account whether the distances between these land uses (e.g., hazardous industrial and residential land uses) are adequate and adhere to national legislation and zoning controls. For incompatible new land uses, the proposal must be either abandoned, or changed by investigating how to reduce the potential risks and effects associated with hazardous activities in the area of interest.

III. Examples of planning approaches and technical risk assessments in member States

54. In UNECE countries, there are different land-use planning approaches based on the methods described in section II.B (or a combination of these). This chapter presents examples of land-use planning approaches in selected countries that have a well-established framework for considering industrial accidents in land-use planning.

A. Approach of the Flanders Region of Belgium

55. In the Flanders Region of Belgium, the regional authorities are responsible for land-use planning policies. There are three tiers of government: regional, provincial and local (municipal), as shown in figure 5.

Figure 5 - Structure and interaction of land-use planning

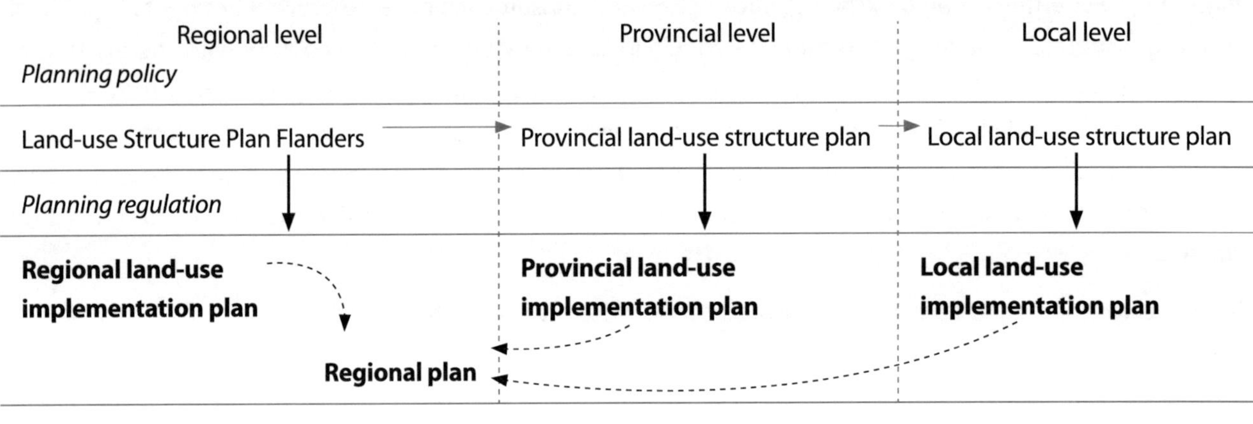

56. The regulations on land-use planning include a large part of the Seveso III Directive and contain provisions for external human safety (i.e., for people outside the boundaries of the facility), such as environmental impact and safety reporting and spatial safety reporting. For upper-tier Seveso facilities, the proponent prepares an environmental safety report for the siting of new or modified hazardous facilities, as part of the environmental permit application. The Safety Reporting Service is the competent authority to approve or reject the environmental safety report. For new developments in the vicinity of Seveso facilities (both lower-tier and upper-tier), advice on external human safety is provided by the Safety Reporting Service, which may request that a spatial safety report be prepared by the competent authority for land-use planning.

57. In addition, the Belgian Cooperation Agreement[10] incorporates a large part of the Seveso Directive into Belgian law. This Agreement includes provisions on safety reports about Seveso facilities.

---

10 Cooperation Agreement between the Federal State, the Communities and the Regions on the representation of the Kingdom of Belgium in the Council of Ministers of the European Union

1. Risk analysis

58. A risk-based approach is used in risk assessment and land-use planning. A quantitative risk assessment is conducted for accident scenarios covering lethality to humans by inhalation of toxic substances, heat radiation of fires, or overpressure effects of explosions.

59. To start with, annual probabilities of accident occurrence are mapped as iso-risk contours[11] and a societal risk curve is calculated for each upper-tier Seveso facility. For the societal risk curve, external people include workers (outside the boundary of the facility), residents, people in traffic and in recreational areas and others nearby. Their estimated presence (in time) on an annual basis is taken into account and the numbers of people indoors and outdoors are treated separately.

60. The methodology for the quantitative risk assessment includes the frequency of failures (that trigger accidents), meteorological conditions, models for effect calculations and damage models for humans.[12]

2. Acceptance criteria for the calculated external human risks

61. The risk criteria for external human risks are as follows:

    a. Local risk based on iso-risk contours (see table 2). Residential areas relate to land with residential zoning and groups of at least five dwellings in non-residential zoning. Areas with vulnerable people are schools, hospitals and retirement homes, which are designed with a higher level of safety;

    b. Societal risk curve (see figure 6).

62. The acceptance criterion takes into account not only the above-mentioned areas, but also other areas, which are included in the societal risk curve in the quantitative risk assessment, in particular:

    a. Public use buildings and areas, where the average presence is at least 200 people per day or 1,000 at peak times;

    b. Major transport routes and air traffic;

    c. External sources of danger, such as pipelines, wind turbines, high-voltage lines and liquefied petroleum gas filling stations.

3. Siting of a new Seveso facility or modification of a Seveso facility

63. The siting or modification of an upper-tier Seveso facility requires the preparation by the proponent of an environmental permit application, including an environmental safety report. The Safety Reporting Service can approve or reject the report based on its content or the quantitative risk assessment.

64. For lower-tier facilities, the licensing authority reviews the safety aspects and can require the proponent to prepare a safety study to examine the risks of the facility against the risk criteria.

65. If determined that the facility complies with the risk criteria, an environmental permit is issued. Where the risk criteria are exceeded, the licensing authority can reject the application or impose special permit conditions, such as the reduction of hazardous substances or additional safety measures (e.g., full containment tanks instead of regular ones).

---

11 Iso-risk contours are calculated for probabilities that are expressed in standard index form, for example, 10^{-6} means one in a million.

12 Damage to human beings is calculated using probit functions, these being quantile functions associated with the normal distribution.

Evaluation on location	Iso-risk contours (per year)
Border of the facility	10^{-5}
Border of residential area	10^{-6}
Border of area containing vulnerable location	10^{-7}

Figure 6 - Societal risk curve showing criterion (in red) and an example probability curve for causalities (blue)

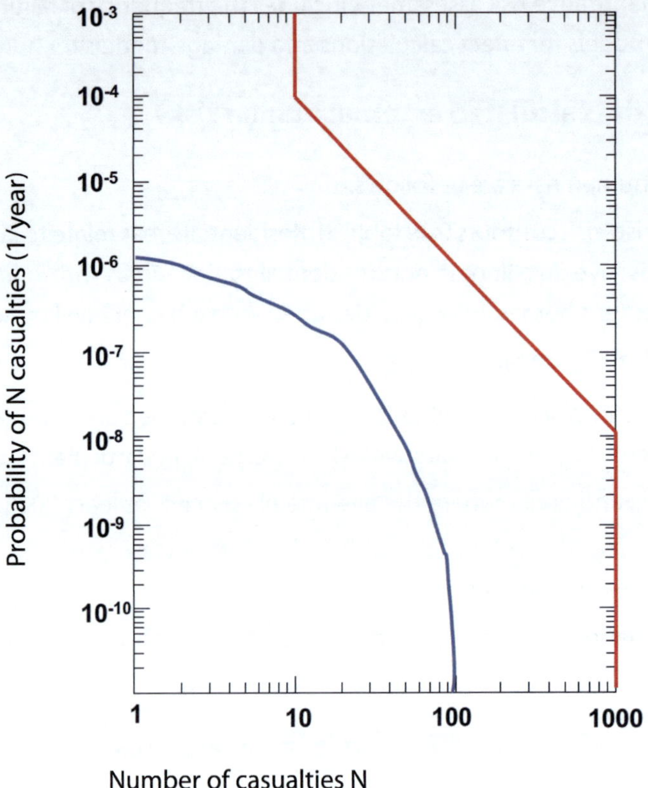

4. Land-use planning

Advice on land-use implementation plans and planning permits

66. Any new land-use implementation plan must be submitted by the land-use planning authority to the Safety Reporting Service for a review of the safety aspects of land-use changes near a hazardous activity. The Safety Reporting Service decides whether: (a) a spatial safety report should be drawn up; (b) a modification to the urban planning regulations should be undertaken; or (c) nothing more needs be done. The decision on whether a new spatial safety report is required depends on whether areas of special attention are within 2 kilometres of a Seveso site and whether the risks are already known.

67. For areas that are not part of a land-use implementation plan, the Safety Reporting Service can provide advice.

Spatial safety reports

68. The spatial safety report contains a description of the proposed development, the site and surroundings, the land-use implementation plan, the quantitative risk assessment, the description of preventive and mitigation measures, and the evaluation of the calculated human risks against the risk acceptance criteria.

69. For new Seveso facilities, a risk-zoning map is prepared based on a variation of the quantitative risk assessment methodology, taking into account land within a 2-kilometre radius. In addition, a safety-zoning map of the area can be prepared, with iso-risk contours of 10^{-6} per year and 10^{-7} per year, showing where no residential areas and no areas with vulnerable people, respectively, are allowed.

70. For a new development for vulnerable people near Seveso facilities, the spatial safety report indicates the risk contour of 10^{-7} per year, where no areas with vulnerable people are allowed. If necessary, it can also provide proposals for safety measures to be fulfilled by existing facilities, such as the provision of water curtains to reduce exposure to a toxic gas, or no glass windows facing the direction of Seveso facilities in buildings with vulnerable people.

B. Approach of France

71. The Toulouse disaster in 2001, which caused 31 fatalities, over 3,000 injuries and damages estimated at €3 billion, has led to a new French land-use planning approach considering the occurrence probability of representative scenarios and a need to act on existing installations. Following this disaster, the French legislation was strengthened, particularly on the siting of hazardous facilities, new urban developments in their vicinity and the flow of information between operators, relevant authorities and the local community.

72. Under the new laws, all possible accident scenarios (a consequence-based approach) at a hazardous facility must be studied and their probabilities of occurrence (a risk-based approach) must be estimated in order to achieve an acceptable safety level. To achieve this, the new regulation sets three requirements:

    a. Harmonizing the risk assessment approaches;

    b. Integrating the risk-based and consequence-based approaches;

    c. Identifying corrective actions for existing or developing urban areas near hazardous facilities and controlling future developments through land-use planning.

73. To address the above requirements, technological risk prevention plans were introduced to develop and manage land-use planning.

74. Furthermore, safety reports must be prepared and contain the following information:

    a. Description of the process and equipment;

    b. Identification of risk sources;

    c. Characterization of the main hazards, based on an estimate of the consequences of instantaneous release of energy and/or toxic substances;

    d. Reduction of hazards based on technical and economic analysis;

    e. Analysis of similar past accidents to identify counter-measures and lessons learned;

    f. Identification of the most critical events through a preliminary risk assessment;

    g. Detailed risk assessment, to assess the impact due to component failure or human error;

    h. Use of mathematical models to estimate the intensity of effects;

    i. Assessment of the probability of accidents and fault protection systems;

    j. Assessment of the potential fatalities and injuries per accident;

    k. Classification of accident scenarios using the national risk acceptability matrix (later used for land-use planning purposes).

75. The safety report provides the basis for societal and individual risk assessments. The societal risk is assessed using a risk matrix. Individual risk is established using alert level maps, which help set up the technological risk prevention plans for land-use planning. The risk assessment is based on the following key elements:

    a. Risk of accident assessment, based on:

        i. Gravity (the intensity or magnitude of the effects), determined by combining the intensity of the effects on the population with the number of people exposed (see table 3) and the number of potential fatalities for each type of effect (see table 4);

        ii. Probability of the accident occurring, calculated using a semi-quantitative approach based on reliability models, such as fault trees (quantitative) and past events and the frequency classes shown in table 5 (qualitative);

        iii. Kinetics (the swiftness of the effects, referring to the time available to respond to the accident with emergency measures), classified as either fast or slow (e.g., an explosion is fast, whereas a toxic release is slow);

    b. Risk acceptability, based on the criteria established for the maximum level of effects that are deemed acceptable. For a given accident, determining the frequency class and gravity level parameters is necessary to identify the risk level according to the national risk acceptability matrix illustrated in table 6.

76. Following the risk assessment above, the alert level concept is applied to determine, for each accident scenario:

    a. Zoning (which provides land-use planning and development controls), based on the four zones in table 7;

    b. Land-use compatibility, based on the probability that a hazardous phenomenon generates effects (i) of a given intensity, (ii) over a certain period of time and (iii) at a given point within the area, using a combination of the probability from the frequency class (table 5), the alert level and the zoning from table 7 (an example is provided in table 8);

    c. Alert-level mapping, based on the zoning and land-use compatibility above (see figure 7).

Table 3 - Intensity of the effects on population

Effects on population	Fire (Continuous thermal radiation in kilowatts per square metre)	Explosion (overpressure)	Toxic release (individual risk)
5% lethal effects	8 kW/m^2	200 mbar	Lethal concentration 5%
1% lethal effects	5 kW/m^2	140 mbar	Lethal concentration 1%
Irreversible effects	3 kW/m^2	50 mbar	Irreversible Effects Threshold
Indirect effects	—	20 mbar	—

Note: Percentages represent the proportion of the population exposed that will suffer lethal effects.

Table 4 - Gravity levels expressed in relation to the number of people exposed

Gravity level	5% lethal effects	1% lethal effects	Irreversible effects
Disastrous	more than 10	more than 100	more than 1000
Catastrophic	1–10	10–100	100–1000
Major	1	1–10	10–100
Serious	0	1	1–10
Moderate	0	0	Less than 1

Frequency class	Qualitative frequency		Quantitative frequency	Semi-quantitative frequency
E	Extremely unlikely scenario	Possible considering current knowledge, but never occurred anywhere worldwide	less than 10^{-5} event/year	
D	Realistic but unlikely scenario	Possible but never occurred in a similar facility	less than 10^{-4} event/year	
C	Improbable scenario	Already occurred in a similar facility worldwide	less than 10^{-3} event/year	A hybrid risk-based model that takes into account factors/ measures reducing the level of risk
B	Probable scenario	Already occurred (or supposed to have occurred) during the lifetime of the facility	less than 10^{-2} event/year	
A	Frequent scenario	Already occurred (several times) during the lifetime of the facility	less than 10^{-1} event/year	

Table 6 - French national risk acceptability matrix for land-use planning evaluations and restrictions in relation to the presence of hazardous activities

Gravity level	Frequency class				
	E	D	C	B	A
Disastrous	NO MMR2	NO	NO	NO	NO
Catastrophic	MMR1	MMR2	NO	NO	NO
Major	MMR1	MMR1	MMR2	NO	NO
Serious	OK	OK	MMR1	MMR2	NO
Moderate	OK	OK	OK	OK	MMR1

Notes: Red (NO): unacceptable risk; green (OK): acceptable risk, i.e. the hazardous facility can operate without additional safety measures; orange (NO for the future / MMR2 for the existing buildings): no more than five dangerous phenomena can be placed in these cells after the operator has taken all measures to reduce the risk; yellow (MMR1): a permit to operate a hazardous facility can be issued after all practicable safety measures have been implemented.

Table 7 - Zoning criteria in the national guide for technological risk prevention plans

Regulated zones	Future land-use planning and construction measures	Possible real estate measures
Dark red	Ban on new construction	Expropriations, relinquishment
Light red	Ban on new construction but possibly allows extending industrial buildings and infrastructure if the necessary safety measures are implemented	Relinquishment
Dark blue	New construction possible depending upon the limitations in their use or implemented safety measures	Compulsory protection measures for housing
Light blue	New construction possible depending upon minor limitations in their use. No public buildings which are difficult to evacuate	Compulsory protection measures for housing

Note: Relinquishment refers to the legal approach whereby homeowners or business owners can abandon their property for the benefit of the authorities who acquire it. In case of non-use of this right, homeowners have to realize compulsory protection measures for housing.

Table 8 - General rules for land-use compatibility for the zones around the hazardous facility

Maximum effects on population at a given point	5% lethal effects			1% lethal effects			Irreversible effects		Indirect effects	
Cumulative probability distribution of dangerous phenomenon at a given point	greater than D	5E to D	less than 5E	greater than D	5E to D	less than 5E	greater than D	5E to D	less than 5E	All
Alert level	Very High (+) VH+	Very High VH	High (+) H+		High H	Medium (+) M+		Medium M	Low	
Zone regulation for thermal radiation and toxic exposure effects	Dark red		Light red			Dark blue		Light blue		
Zone regulation for overpressure effects	Dark red		Light red				Dark blue		Light blue	

Notes: VH+ and VH: any existing houses can be subject to compulsory purchase (i.e. expropriation) or relinquishment. H+ and H: areas subject to relinquishment. VH+ to H: development of new buildings (i.e. residential or services) are generally not allowed. M+ to M (toxicity or heat radiation) and M+ to Low (overpressure): development is subject to special conditions. 5E: the probability of five extremely unlikely scenarios (see table 5).

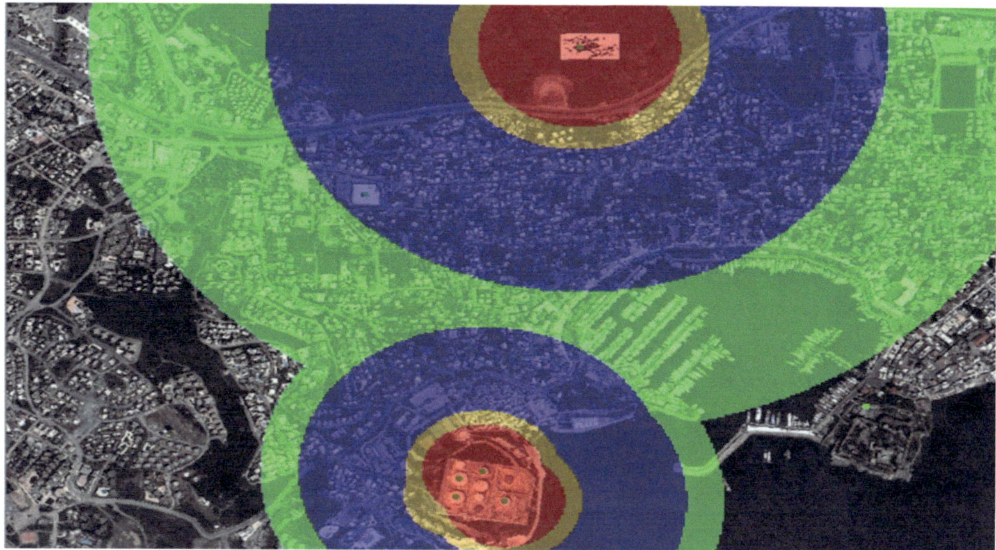

Source: Major Accident Hazards Bureau, European Commission Joint Research Centre.

77. For each one of the three effects (thermal radiation, overpressure and toxic exposures), an alert level map is created showing three contours representing the intensity of the effects on the exposed population (i.e., 5% lethal effect, 1% lethal effect and irreversible damage). A land-use compatibility criterion is obtained by overlapping all alert level maps referring to the same effect and calculating the frequencies of occurrence of these accidents. This can lead to an increase of alert level for a certain location.[13]

C. Approach of Italy

78. National laws are implemented by the Italian regions through their own legislation, which addresses issues of major-accident hazards, industrial safety, public health and safety, civil protection, natural resources protection and regional economic development.

79. The decree on minimal safety requirements for urban and territorial planning in areas subject to major accident risks[14] requires that adequate safety distances (a deterministic approach) be established between hazardous facilities and residential areas regarding:

    a.   Construction of new facilities;

    b.   Enlargement of existing facilities;

    c.   New developments close to a facility.

80. The Italian land-use planning approach is semi-quantitative and is centred on three stages as described in the decree:[15,16]

    a.   Identifying vulnerable territorial and environmental elements near the hazardous facility;

---

13 For example, 10 accident scenarios of class E count as one D. Slow accident effects are calculated separately.

14 Ministry of Public Works, 'Minimum safety requirements with regard to urban and regional planning for areas affected by major accident hazards establishments', published in the Official Journal, n.138 (16 June 2001). Available from http://www.mit.gov.it/mit/media/seveso2/pages/documents/nazionali/DM090501.pdf.

15 See Italy, Ministry of Infrastructure and Transport, 'Territorial government and technological risk, intervention methodologies and experiences of implementation of the ministerial decree of 9 May 2001'. Available (in Italian) from http://www.mit.gov.it/mit/media/seveso2/pages/documents/libro_edizione_2/indice.htm (accessed on 16 September 2016).

16 A. Carpignano, G. Pignatta and A. Spaziante, "Land use planning around Seveso II installations: the Italian approach", *Proceedings of the European Conference on Safety and Reliability*, 16–20 September 2001, Torino, Italy, p. 1763.

b. Determining the impact area following an accident;

c. Evaluating the territorial and environmental compatibility with the hazardous facility.

Step 1: identifying vulnerable territorial and environmental elements

Vulnerable territorial elements

81. Areas of land are categorized into six classes according to an urbanization or construction index and community-related characteristics (see table 9). The categorization takes into account the difficulty in evacuating:

a. Vulnerable people such as children, the elderly and the sick;

b. Residents in five (or more) storey buildings and crowds in public spaces;

c. Residents in isolated or low-rise buildings;

d. People undertaking low-vulnerability activities (characterized by short-term presence of people);

e. People undertaking high-vulnerability outdoor activities.

Table 9 - Six classes of land categorization

Category	Type of land-use development
A	Residential (building land index over 4.5 m³/m²)
	Developments accommodating people with limited mobility (e.g., hospitals, nursing homes, schools or kindergartens (over 25 beds or 100 people present))
	Places subject to outdoor overcrowding, e.g., fixed marketplaces or retail stores (over 500 people)
B	Residential (building land index between 4.5 and 1.5 m³/m²)
	Developments accommodating people with limited mobility, such as hospitals, nursing homes, schools or kindergartens (over 25 beds or 100 people present)
	Places subject to outdoor overcrowding (up to 500 people)
	Places subject to indoor overcrowding, e.g., shopping centres, offices, schools, universities (over 500 people)
	Areas subject to significant overcrowding, e.g., public entertainment, sport, cultural or religious sites (over 100 people outdoors, or 1,000 indoors)
	Railway stations and other transport nodes (over 1,000 people/day)
C	Residential (building land index between 1.5 and 1m³/m²)
	Places subject to indoor overcrowding (up to 500 people)
	Areas subject to significant overcrowding (up to 100 people outdoors or 1,000 indoors)
	Railway stations and other transport nodes (up to 1,000 people/day)
D	Residential (building land index between 1 and 0.5 m³/m²)
	Areas subject to significant overcrowding on a monthly basis e.g. fairs, open-air markets, cemeteries
E	Predominantly residential (building land index over 0.5 m³/m²)
	Industries and agricultural, manufacturing and livestock enterprises
F	Hazardous facility area
	Area adjacent to the hazardous facility where no industrial elements or activities and people are present

Note: Amounts expressed in m³/m² indicate the total volume of buildings expressed in cubic metres divided by the area expressed in square metres.

82. Vulnerable environmental elements are identified by assessing the potential environmental damage based on the release of dangerous substances and the type of accident (e.g., the effects of an explosion on water or subsoil may be negligible, whereas the effects of toxic gas dispersion on vegetation must be considered). These elements include:

    a. Landscape and environmental heritage assets;

    b. Natural protected areas;

    c. Surface water resources;

    d. Protected or unprotected groundwater resources;

    e. Agricultural land use.

Step 2: Determining the impact area following an accident

83. Accident consequence models are applied to estimate the level of damage to people and structures for each type of effect, that is, thermal radiation, overpressure and toxic concentration. The damage thresholds values presented in table 10 are defined by the decree. The impact is identified by:

    a. Comparing the calculated damage in the affected area with the threshold values and representing the results on a map;

    b. Overlapping the impact map with the map showing vulnerable territorial and environmental elements.

84. The frequency of occurrence of an accident event is associated with one of four probability classes (see table 11, first column).

Table 10 - Threshold values adopted in the Italian regulation

Accident type	Elevated fatalities	Start fatalities	Permanent injuries	Reversible injuries	Structural damage
Fire *(stationary thermal radiation)*	12.5 kW/m²	7 kW/m²	5 kW/m²	3 kW/m²	12.5 kW/m²
Boiling liquid expanding vapour explosion or fireball *(variable thermal radiation)*	Fireball radius	359 kJ/m²	200 kJ/m²	125 kJ/m²	200–800 m (storage tank type)
Flash fire *(instantaneous thermal radiation)*	Lower flammable limit	0.5 Lower flammable limit	—	—	—
Vapour cloud explosion *(peak overpressure)*	0.3 bar (0.6 bar open space)	0.14 bar	0.07 bar	0.03 bar	0.3 bar
Toxic release *(absorbed dose)*	Lethal concentration for 50% (30 minute exposure)	—	Immediately dangerous to life or health	—	—

Step 3: Evaluating the territorial and environmental compatibility

Territorial compatibility

85. The compatibility of the zones surrounding a hazardous facility is evaluated by means of a qualitative compatibility risk matrix presented in table 11.

Table 11 - Compatibility matrix for land uses A–F (table 9)

Probability class (events/year)	Consequence category			
	Reversible injuries	Permanent injuries	Start fatalities	Elevated fatalities
less than 10^{-6}	ABCDEF	BCDEF	CDEF	DEF
10^{-4}–10^{-6}	BCDEF	CDEF	DEF	EF
10^{-3}–10^{-4}	CDEF	DEF	EF	F
greater than 10^{-3}	DEF	EF	F	F

86. The process for mapping the territorial compatibility around a hazardous facility is as follows:

   a. Select an accident event (fire, explosion or toxic dispersion);

   b. Calculate the frequency of occurrence and select the probability class;

   c. Calculate the effects in each point of the area (high or starting lethality and irreversible or reversible effects);

   d. Identify the compatible building categories by using the compatibility matrix;

   e. Repeat the above steps for each accident event;

   f. Select the most restrictive compatibility level for each point of the area.

Environmental compatibility

87. Land-use planning and risk evaluation must take into account the specific environmental context of hazardous facilities (e.g., seismic and hydrological areas).

88. The classification of environmental damage is related to the potential release of dangerous substances and is defined by considering:

   a. Quantity and characteristics of the substances released;

   b. Specific measures applied to reduce and mitigate the environmental impacts.

89. Two environmental categories are then defined:

   a. Significant damage, for example, whereby remediation and environmental restoration of sites can be completed within the space of two years;

   b. Serious damage, for example, whereby remediation and environmental restoration of sites will require more than two years.

90. Serious environmental damage is always considered incompatible. For significant damage, prevention and mitigation measures should be applied.

Operating permits procedure

91. The permit is issued by the regional authorities (responsible for lower-tier Seveso facilities) and the Regional Technical Committee (responsible for upper-tier facilities).

92. The public concerned can consult the safety report of the hazardous facility and the technical report on land-use planning (excluding industrial, commercial, personal, public security or national defence information). The consultation procedures are defined by the planning regulation and the consultation period starts after the publication of an urban plan in the official journal.

D. Approach of the United Kingdom

93. In the United Kingdom, England, Scotland, Wales and Northern Ireland each have their own land-use planning regulations. The planning authorities of each country are responsible for implementing the land-use planning aspects of the Seveso III Directive. The two Health and Safety Executives in Great Britain (England, Scotland and Wales) and Northern Ireland are the bodies responsible for implementing the Seveso III Directive by regulating major accident hazard facilities through the Control of Major Accident Hazards process and providing guidance to local planning authorities on land-use compatibility near hazardous facilities.

94. Local planning authorities are responsible for defining land-use planning and environmental management. They must consult HSE for any development plan regarding hazard facilities and areas that fall within the consultation distance (a deterministic approach). In this context HSE developed an online planning advice app,[17] which is available to local planning authorities and developers for pre-planning advice on territorial compatibility. The local planning authorities may refuse negative advice from HSE as its advice is not legally binding. However, the Executive can ask the Secretary of State to override the decisions of planning authorities when considering developments near hazardous facilities.

1. For proposed hazardous facilities

95. There are two processes that HSE conducts: first. the inspection of safety reports to check that operators have demonstrated compliance with the requirements of the Seveso III Directive; and. second, risk assessments of Hazardous Substances Consent applications (for a planning permit to have hazardous substances on-site up to a requested maximum quantity) made by operators to planning authorities. The HSE assessment of Hazardous Substances Consent applications is undertaken separately from assessments of safety reports produced under the Control of Major Accident Hazards for upper-tier Seveso facilities.

96. HSE assesses an application for Hazardous Substances Consent to establish a consultation zone (or distance) around the hazardous facility. The consultation zones represent potentially significant consequences for human health, urban areas and major transport routes. The zone boundaries are derived using the criteria in table 12. In terms of individual risk from toxic release to a hypothetical house resident:

   a. A risk of 10^{-5} per year of a dangerous dose or worse (implying that vulnerable people are at a risk of death of about 10 in a million per year) is used to advise against proposed development cases that are above a certain size;[18]

   b. 10^{-6} per year of a dangerous dose or worse is another boundary that is used;

   c. $0.3.10^{-6}$ per year of a dangerous dose or worse is the boundary used to advise against developments, of a certain size, for vulnerable people.

---

17 Available from http://www.hse.gov.uk/landuseplanning/planning-advice-web-app.htm (accessed 31 August 2016).

18 See HSE Land Use Planning Methodology, available from http://www.hse.gov.uk/landuseplanning/methodology.htm.

Table 12 - Criteria for the definition of consultation zones around the facility

Consultation zone	Fire (thermal radiation consequences)	Explosion (overpressure consequences)	Toxic release (Residual Individual risk of dangerous dose or worse to a hypothetical house resident)
Inner	1800 TDU	600 mbar	greater than 10^{-5}
Middle	1000 TDU	140 mbar	10^{-5}–10^{-6}
Outer	500 TDU	70 mbar	10^{-6}–3.10^{-7}

Note: TDU, or Thermal Dose Unit = 1 $(kW/m^2)^{4/3}$s.

97. HSE is not consulted beyond the outer zones. An example of three consultation zones obtained for a toxic release is shown in figure 8. Following the 2005 Buncefield disaster,[19] HSE introduced a fourth consultation zone for large-scale petrol storage sites.[20]

98. To check the compatibility of an application for Hazardous Substances Consent with the surrounding population, HSE follows its Planning Case and Assessment Guide.

Figure 8 - Three consultation zones and their individual risk consultation zones for toxic releases around hazardous facility

Consultation distance boundary

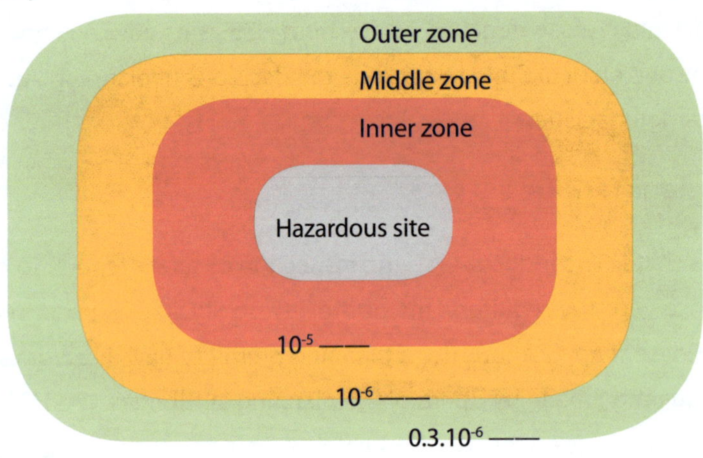

Source: Lorenzo van Wijk.

2. For new developments within the vicinity of existing hazardous facilities

99. For making decisions on proposed developments near existing hazardous facilities, HSE established a procedure to assess the compatibility of developments proposed within the consultation zones, which includes:

    a. Vulnerability of the exposed population;

    b. Proportion of time spent by any individual in the development;

    c. Size of the building or infrastructure;

    d. People dwelling indoors or outdoors;

---

19 United Kingdom, Control of Major Accident Hazards report, "Buncefield: Why did it happen?". Available from http://www.hse.gov.uk/comah/buncefield/buncefield-report.pdf.

20 For large-scale petrol storage tanks, a development proximity zone is defined within 150 metres of the tank farm bund, the inner zone up to 250 metres, the middle zone up to 300 metres and the outer zone up to 400 metres. See also the HSE report, "Land use planning advice around large scale petrol storage sites" (version 2). Available from http://www.hse.gov.uk/foi/internalops/hid_circs/technical_general/spc_tech_gen_43/.

e. Ease of evacuation or other emergency measures;

f. Characteristics of buildings (number of storeys).

100. Based on these factors, HSE defined five vulnerability levels (see table 13).

101. An advice matrix is obtained by coupling the land-use development category with a vulnerability level and attributing this combination with a consultation zone (e.g., in table 13). The advice is one factor for consideration when making planning decisions.

102. Inside the inner zone, industrial activities and parking lots are allowed. Residential buildings are allowed within the middle zone provided the developments do not include vulnerable centres such as schools and hospitals. Residential areas and small vulnerable centres are allowed within the outer zone. Finally, in the case of large-scale petrol storage sites, unoccupied developments within the development proximity zone are allowed. No restrictions are imposed beyond the outer consultation zone.

3. Access to information

103. The HSE assessment reports are not published, contrary to the practices in France and Italy. However, operators must provide all relevant information on existing safety measures at the facility and the external emergency measures in the event of an accident, without being requested, to the people potentially affected. Land-use planning risk maps can be provided upon request. Some local planning authorities publish consultation zones in their local plans.

104. The public must be consulted on the adoption of a local plan. The local plan application and all other relevant information is made available to the public and planning meetings are held. The public is entitled and given adequate opportunity to express its opinions on the local plans, which the local planning authority must take into consideration. Individual planning applications, including applications for Hazardous Substances Consent, are also subject to public notification and review.

105. Separately, the environmental agencies advise on environmental impacts. The local planning authorities consult the separate environmental agencies in England, Wales, Scotland and Northern Ireland, as the HSE role is to provide advice on the risk aspects to the public.

Table 13 - Health and Safety Executive advice matrix for proposed developments around a hazardous facility

Vulnerability level	Land-use developments (examples)	Outer zone	Middle zone	Inner zone	Development proximity zone
0	Developments usually unoccupied (e.g., long-term parking, storage facilities)	DAA	DAA	DAA	DAA
1	Workplace buildings with less than 100 occupants and less than 3 occupied storeys, and stand-alone car parks (e.g., factories, warehouses and offices)	DAA	DAA	DAA	AA
2	Residential areas of up to 30 dwelling units at a density of no more than 40 units per hectare. Hotels up to 100 beds, camping up to 33 pitches	DAA	DAA	AA	AA
3	Indoor public spaces with over 5,000 m² total floor space (e.g., retail and leisure centres). Outdoor public spaces with over 100 people but up to 1,000 at any one time	DAA	AA	AA	AA
4	Highly vulnerable or very large facilities (e.g., hospital or nursing home larger than 0.25 hectares, school larger than 1.4 hectares and stadium)	AA	AA	AA	AA

Abbreviations: DAA = Do not Advise Against development, AA = Advise Against development

IV. Conclusion

106. The present technical guidance provides examples of land-use planning approaches, risk assessment methods and the key steps in evaluating and making decisions on land-use policies, plans, programmes and projects involving hazardous facilities and their potential effects on human health, property and the environment.

107. The previous chapters have highlighted that:

    a. Land-use planning is a necessary process whereby land is allocated and regulated for different socioeconomic activities, including hazardous activities;

    b. Land-use planning controls should aim to create safe and sustainable environments by setting procedures for identifying, assessing and managing all sources of risk to human health and the environment;

    c. When developing or making decisions on national land-use policies, plans, programmes or projects, the proponents, authorities, stakeholders and decision makers should take into account:

        i. The location, safety aspects and risks associated with existing and proposed hazardous activities,

        ii. The relevant provisions and procedures of the Industrial Accidents Convention and UNECE safety guidelines developed under the Convention (listed in section I.B);

    d. Different planning approaches and risk assessment methods are used to identify, assess and manage the safety and risk aspects (including transboundary risks and effects) of hazardous facilities;

    e. The potential effects of a proposal on human health, environment and property should be based on the evaluation of the risk assessment and mapping against the compatibility and risk acceptability criteria.